T0021308

Diamond Sky

Series Ganesha Press

ABOUT GANESHA PRESS
Ganesha Press is the publishing house of Dechen, an
international association of Sakya and Kagyu Buddhist
centres and groups founded by Lama Jampa Thaye under
the authority of Karma Thinley Rinpoche.

Other books by Lama Jampa Thaye

A Garland of Gold
Way of Tibetan Buddhism
Wisdom in Exile
Rain of Clarity
River of Memory: Dharma Chronicles

Diamond Sky

Preparing for Vajrayana

Lama Jampa Thaye

RABSEL
PUBLICATIONS

DIAMOND SKY: Preparing for Vajrayana
Copyright © 2023 Ganesha Press Limited

Illustrations by Rana Lister

First printed in the UK by Ganesha Press. This edition by Rabsel Publications in
partnership with Ganesha Press and Dechen Foundation Books.

GANESHA PRESS
121 Sommerville Road, St Andrews, Bristol, BS6 5BX, UK

RABSEL PUBLICATIONS
16, rue de Babylone
76430 La Remuée, France
www.rabsel.com
contact@rabsel.com

© Rabsel Publications, La Remuée, France, 2023
ISBN 978-2-36017-055-5

To my masters

Contents

འཇམ་དཔ་སྐྱིད་ལ་ཉོག་ལྱར་ལེགས་ཚོགས་དུ་མས་མཐོ་བའི་དཔྱེན་
ཡུལ་རྒྱལ་ཁམས་ཉེན་པོ་ནས། དྱ་བརྟེན་ཉིས་རབ་ཀྱི་ཕྱོགས་དཔལ་མཐའ་བ། རང་སྒོབ་
ལྱགས་པ་གྱམས་པ་མཐུན་ཡམས་ཀྱིས་བརྩེ་མས་མཛད་པའི་ཌི་དམ་པའི་ཚོམ་ལ་འཇུག་
པའི་རྒྱལ་འདིས། ༞ སྐྱེན་པ་སྱབ་པའི་དཔར་པོའི་རི་ལྱགས་ལ་མ་བརང་པོ་ལ་སྐྱེན་
གཉེར་བུ་རྒྱུའི་བསྐལ་པ་བརང་པོ་རྩན་ལ་དོར་མ་ནོར་པའི་མི་ག་སྱེ་བའི་ཡིད་ཚེས་ཡོད་
པར་འགྱུར་གྱིས་ཚོན་བརྩིན་རྒྱུ་བ་གལ་ཆེ་ལ། ཚེས་པའང་འདི་ལྱར་དགོས་ཤེས་སྒོ་
ཚོན་རྒྱམས་པ་གང་ནས་གཉུང་བསྐྱལ་རོ། མདོ་ཁམས་ཚོས་ཀྱི་ཞིང་ཁར་སྱེས་
པའི་བསྐལ་པ་དགེ་བ་ཅན། སྐྱེན་དང་བསྱན་པ་ལ་མི་ཉེད་པའི་དང་གུང་རང་ལྱན་པ།
༞ མ་ཚོན་ཁ་ཚོད་པར་འཆང་བའི་ལྱང་གིས་ཀཀྲ་སྱིན་ལས་བཞི་མེང་པས། རབ་གྱུ་
འཕྱ་བཅུན་པའི་རྱ་ཚེས་དགེ་བར་བྱིན་

Preface
by Karma Thinley Rinpoche

This method of entering the holy dharma has been composed by my student the tantrika Jampa Thaye, who is endowed with the glorious power of faith, energy and wisdom and comes from the kingdom of Great Britain, a country elevated through its many excellent qualities to resemble the peak of the world. Since those who have the good fortune of training in the excellent path of the tradition of Buddha Shakyamuni presented here will come to possess the eye of conviction which discriminates the unmistaken meaning, it is important that everyone should endeavour to study this teaching. Thus I request.

At the urging of my representative Jampa, I, who have the virtuous good fortune of being born in the dharma country of Kham and possess undivided faith and devotion towards Lord Buddha and his doctrine, named the Fourth Karma Thinley by the authority of the one who holds the black crown, have written this at an auspicious date in the seventeenth cycle.

Introduction

Many years ago, the first edition of this work was published as a brief guide to the core practices of the three 'vehicles' of Buddhism—Shravakayana, Mahayana and Vajrayana. Now, this new edition from Rabsel Publications gives me the opportunity to revisit this material and expand it a little. That being so, it might be useful to say something here about the contents of the book by way of an introduction to its six chapters.

Since it is our connection with continuing lines of spiritual transmission which makes it possible for us to travel the Buddhist path, confidence that these lineages are authentic and unbroken is of great importance. Consequently, Chapter One, 'Discovering the Things that Remain', presents a concise history of the dharma in India and Tibet, whence it is now spreading to the West.

Chapter Two, 'A Solid Rock', explores the act of taking refuge by which we actually enter the Buddhist path and analyses the significance and nature of 'the Three Jewels'—the Buddha, the dharma and the sangha. It also discusses the role of the lama or spiritual master, who is regarded as a fourth object of refuge in Vajrayana.

However, although one might make a formal connection to dharma through taking refuge, one might still be held captive by worldly ambitions and activities, an eventuality which would render our dharma practice fruitless. The only antidote to such seduction is the cultivation of a sense of disillusionment or renunciation. Consequently, in Chapter Three, 'Tasting Birth and Death', the series of contemplations known as 'the four thoughts that turn the mind' are presented as the means to generate the requisite renunciation and as the quintessential teachings of the Shravakayana.

Chapters Four and Five, 'Open Heart' and 'The Crystal Key' respectively, focus on bodhichitta ('the thought of enlightenment'), which, as the essence of compassion and wisdom, represents the core of the Mahayana, the Great Vehicle. In particular, 'Open Heart' details how we might develop the compassion that impels us to dedicate ourselves to achieving buddhahood for the benefit of all beings. Yet, this altruism alone, without the wisdom aspect of bodhichitta, cannot lead to buddhahood because one would still be trapped by our erroneous projections. Hence, in the following chapter, 'The Crystal Key', the meditations of calm-abiding and insight are detailed, since it is from these two that the necessary wisdom is born.

Finally, in Chapter Six, 'The Path of the Emperor', the purpose and characteristics of the third vehicle, the Vajrayana, are outlined. As practice of this vehicle is so crucial for the swift attainment of buddhahood, this chapter shows how one might accomplish the various facets of this esoteric system.

I cannot repay the kindness of my own masters, H.H. Sakya Gongma Trichen and Karma Thinley Rinpoche, as well as that shown me by H.H. Karmapa and Ngor Phende Rinpoche, but this book is offered to them. If it has any merit, it is due to them. If there are any errors in it, they are due to me. Thanks also to my wife Albena and my family for their unending support in this work, as in all others, and to Benjamin Lister for his help in preparing this new edition.

Lama Jampa Thaye
London, January 2022

Padmakara

ONE
Discovering the Things that Remain

The Coming of the Buddha

According to the common understanding, the history of Buddhism begins with the south Asian prince, known to his followers as Buddha Shakyamuni ('The Sage of the Shakyas'), who was born some two thousand five hundred years ago in Lumbini, a place situated just inside the present-day borders of Nepal. At the age of thirty-five, he attained enlightenment in Bodhgaya, and then, to share his understanding of the way to liberation, he 'turned the wheel of dharma' in Varanasi and various other places. Finally, at the age of eighty, having spent more than half his life teaching, Shakyamuni passed away in Kushinagara, leaving his followers to collect and disseminate his teachings for the benefit of succeeding generations.

According to the uncommon understanding, as preserved exclusively in the extensive Mahayana sutras and tantras,[1] long before his appearance as Shakyamuni,

9

the Buddha (literally 'the awakened one') achieved enlightenment as Buddha Vairochana ('The Illuminator') in the spiritual realm of Akanistha. There, manifesting the radiant form of the sambhogakaya ('the body of enjoyment'), he constantly bestows teachings on an entourage of bodhisattvas who reside on the highest spiritual level. At the same time, to communicate the dharma to ordinary beings, the Buddha emanates in our world in the magical forms of the nirmanakaya ('the body of emanation'), one such emanation being Shakyamuni, the buddha of our historical period. Thus it is said that, in this particular aeon, one thousand nirmanakayas will manifest and reveal the dharma through twelve archetypal deeds.

These twelve great acts, performed by Shakyamuni and the other nirmanakayas, are delineated in *The Supreme Continuum Treatise* (Skt. *Uttaratantrashastra*) as follows:

> Through the greatest compassion
> He knows the world.
> Having seen all worlds,
> Whilst never departing from the dharmakaya ('the truth body')
> Through various forms, apparitional by nature,
> The one excellently born into the highest birth
> Descends from Tushita,
> Enters the womb and is nobly born.
> Perfectly skilled in all art and craft,
> Taking delight in the company of his consorts,
> He renounces the world and practises austerities.
> Going to the 'heart of enlightenment',
> He vanquishes the hosts of Mara.
> Then—perfect enlightenment—
> He turns the wheel of dharma and passes away into nirvana.[2]

Shakyamuni is the fourth of these buddhas who have been predicted to appear in our world during the present 'fortunate aeon'. However, in actuality, though he has manifested in this way, he, like all buddhas, has never departed from his ultimate mode of being, the dharmakaya, which, arising from the apprehension of the true nature of reality itself, is untouched by birth and death.

The Shravakayana

Following Lord Buddha's passing from our world, his teaching, now gathered in the scriptural collections of the sutras ('discourses'), was preserved in diverse lines of transmission. The first such lines to flourish openly were those espousing the teachings of the Shravakayana ('The Vehicle of the Disciples') or, as it is sometimes known, the Hinayana ('The Lesser Vehicle'). This second name reflects the motivation animating those who upheld these teachings, being the resolve to win only their own liberation from the cycle of birth and death. With this aim in mind, the followers of this system, whether practising in groups of like-minded 'disciples' (Skt. shravaka) or, eschewing companionship, as 'solitary realisers' (Skt. pratyeka-buddha), contemplated such topics as the four noble truths and dependent origination.

Although a total of eighteen Shravaka sects are reported to have existed in India in this early period following the passing of the Buddha, the most important were the Sarvastivada, Sammatiya, Mahasanghika and the Sthaviravada, each of which maintained a particular recension of the collection of the sutras. The first three are now extinct but the latter, known nowadays by its Pali name of Theravada ('The Doctrine of the Elders'), still survives and is, in fact, the dominant form of Buddhism in south-east Asia. However, it was thinkers hailing from the Sarvastivada sect, such as Vasumitra and Kumaralata, who established the two tenet-systems (Skt. siddhanta) known respectively as Vaibhashika ('Differentiators') and Sautrantika ('Sutra Followers'), which, in time, came to represent the philosophical views of the Shravakayana.

The Mahayana

The Mahayana ('The Great Vehicle') teachings were originally delivered in our world by Buddha Shakyamuni to those among his followers who were inspired by the altruistic ideals of the bodhisattva path, on which achieving buddhahood for the benefit of others is proclaimed as the highest good. With such an intention they were following in the steps of the Buddha himself, whose own journey to enlightenment had commenced with this very same motivation. The Mahayana scriptural collection began to spread widely from about the first century C.E. onwards through the dissemination of such sutras as *The Perfection of Wisdom, Ratnakuta, The White Lotus of the True Dharma, Avatamsaka* and others.

The two most important figures in the development of the Mahayana in India were the great philosophers Asanga and Nagarjuna, founders of the Chittamatra and Madhyamaka tenet-systems respectively. Thus Asanga (ca. 3rd–4th centuries C.E.), together with his half-brother Vasubandhu, elaborated the Chittamatra ('Mind Only') system on the basis of such sutras as the *Lankavatara* and *Sandhinirmochana.* In these discourses Lord Buddha had explained how the appearances of the phenomenal world have no other foundation than mind itself. In addition to composing his own treatises expounding this system of thought, such as *Yogacharabhumi* and *Mahayanasamgraha*, Asanga revealed a series of five works received through the inspiration of the bodhisattva Maitreya. These five works, the *Abhisamayalamkara*, *Mahayanasutralamkara*, *Dharmadharmata Vibhaga*, *Madhyanta Vibhaga* and the *Uttaratantrashastra*, were known collectively as '*The Five Teachings of Maitreya*' and have been of great importance for all followers of the Mahayana. Many later scholars such as Gorampa Sonam Sengge (1429–1489) held these works to be a mixture of Chittamatra and Madhyamaka in intent, but others, such as Dolpopa Sherab Gyaltsen (1292–1361) and Karmapa Rangjung Dorje (1284–1339), regarded them as representing the view of the so-called 'Great Madhyamaka'.[3]

Nagarjuna (ca. 1st century C.E.), the other pre-eminent Mahayana figure, developed the Madhyamaka ('Middle Way') tenet-system out of Buddha's teaching on the doctrine of emptiness, the lack of any abiding essence in any phenomena whatsoever, a teaching that had been extensively proclaimed in such sutras as *The Perfection of Wisdom*. Nagarjuna's lineage was continued by his close disciple Aryadeva, who hailed from Shri Lanka. In later centuries two principal branches of the Madhyamaka developed in India: the Svatantrika ('Those who employ syllogisms'), represented by such masters as Bhavaviveka and Jnanagarbha, and the Prasangika ('Consequentialists'), represented by Buddhapalita, Chandrakirti and Shantideva.

The Vajrayana

Following the appearance of the Shravakayana and Mahayana and the flourishing of various Buddhist kingdoms in the Indian sub-continent, a third major wave of Buddhism spread between the fifth and tenth centuries C.E. with the revelation of the Vajrayana ('The Indestructible Vehicle') or 'Secret Mantra' teachings, which had been preserved in the scriptural collection known as 'tantras'. According to tradition, these teachings were first revealed in Akanistha and other pure realms by Buddha appearing in the form known as Vajradhara ('The Holder of the Vajra'), the embodiment of the dharmakaya itself, and were then proclaimed in our world during the lifetime of Shakyamuni. Due to the esoteric nature of these teachings, relatively few followers received them at that time but, nonetheless, their transmission was maintained in such places as Oddiyana and Shambhala, before being brought back to India at a later date.[4]

Since the tantric teaching shares the ethical impulse and philosophical view of the Mahayana and is distinct only in the skilful means of practice that it presents, it is appropriate to characterise this system as the 'Uncommon Mahayana'. In point of fact, when distinguishing these two wings of the Mahayana in such a manner, the Common Mahayana may also be termed either 'The Causal Vehicle' or 'The Perfection Vehicle', while the Uncommon Mahayana may be designated 'The Resultant Vehicle' or 'The Mantra Vehicle'. The significance of such terminology will become clear in later chapters of this present work.

In any event, these tantric or 'Secret Mantra' teachings were preserved in some secrecy until the sixth century C.E., from which time onwards they were revealed somewhat more openly. However, as is evident from religious histories of the time, a certain reserve concerning their transmission was still exercised. In that mediaeval period, the most famous practitioners of the Vajrayana in India were the so-called eighty-four siddhas, which group included such masters of mahamudra[5] as Virupa, Naropa, Saraha, Tilopa and the female siddha Lakshminkara.

The Coming of the Dharma to Tibet and the Nyingma tradition

The transfer of dharma to Tibet from India took place in two phases, known as the periods of the 'early' and 'later' diffusions, during which time the full range of Shravaka, Mahayana and Vajrayana teachings were transmitted to the Tibetans. The early diffusion commenced during the reign of King Songtsen Gampo (d. 649) and came to a climax in the reign of his descendant Trisong Detsen (756–797). At that time, the great Vajrayana master, Padmakara or 'Guru Rinpoche', the 'Precious Lama' from Oddiyana, together with the Indian philosopher and abbot, Shantarakshita, upholder of the hybrid Svatantrika Madhyamaka Yogachara view, established the first Tibetan dharma-centre at Samye, south-west of Lhasa. There they initiated the study and practice of the sutras and tantras.

Furthermore, Padmakara, having transmitted the teachings to his twenty-five foremost disciples, such as his consort Yeshe Tsogyal,[6] from the Kharchen clan, concealed a vast number of esoteric instructions in cypher manuscript form in various places throughout Tibet. These have been discovered at the predicted times through the centuries by blessed and prophesied emanations of Padmakara himself who were subsequently referred to as 'treasure revealers' (Tib. terton).

From the activities of Padmakara and other great eighth century masters, such as the Indian scholar and yogin Vimalamitra and the Tibetan translator Vairochana, sprang the first of the four major schools of Buddhism in Tibet: the Nyingma ('Ancient') tradition. The principal teaching of this tradition is 'The Great Perfection' (Skt. maha sandhi; Tib. dzok chen).[7] Amongst the numerous accomplished Nyingma teachers who have appeared in Tibetan history, perhaps the greatest was Longchen Rabjam (1308–1363), whose numerous works contain the most complete presentation of The Great Perfection. Other celebrated masters of this school included Rikdzin Jatson Nyingpo (1585–1656) and Rikdzin Jigme Lingpa (1729–1797), both of whose cycles of instructions are still popular today.

The Development of the ' New Schools'

The later diffusion of dharma in the eleventh and twelfth centuries followed a period of confusion in Tibetan Buddhism, due largely to the anti-monastic policies of King Langdarma and the subsequent collapse of a centralised monarchy in the mid-ninth century. This second diffusion coincided with, and was to some extent a product of, a series of new translations of tantras from India initiated by such scholars as Lotsava Rinchen Zangpo (958–1055) Drokmi Shakya Yeshe (992–1072) and Marpa Chokyi Lodro (1012–1096). During this period, in addition to a number of lesser sects such as Cho-yul, Shijay, Jonang and Shangpa, three especially prominent schools, all following the so called new tantras, came into being: the Kadam, the Dakpo Kagyu and the Sakya.

The Kadam School

The first of these, the Kadam school, traces its origins to the work of the learned and charismatic Bengali master Atisha (979–1054), who spent the last thirteen years of his life in Tibet. It was Atisha's chief Tibetan disciple Dromton (1000–1064) who actually founded the sect and its first monastery at Radeng in 1060, ensuring that, henceforth, the school would be exclusively monastic. Subsequently, the Kadampa teachings spread through central and western Tibet. The key teachings of the tradition were transmitted in three lines: (i) 'treatises' (Tib. *zhung*) consisting of six classical texts, such as Shantideva's *Entering the Bodhisattva Conduct*; (ii) 'oral instructions' (Tib. *damnag*) consisting of the mind-training (Tib. *lojong*) meditation cycle; and (iii) 'pith-instructions' (Tib. *mennag*) comprising tantric teachings such as the famous *Four Deities of the Kadam*: Shakyamuni, Avalokiteshvara (Tib. *Chenrezik*), Green Tara and Achala.

The Kadam alone, of the major new schools, has not survived as an independent sect, although its teachings have been absorbed into the other traditions of Tibetan Buddhism. In this respect, in the late fourteenth century Tsongkhapa Lozang Drakpa from Amdo (1357–1419) established the Gelug school or, as it was sometimes styled 'the new Kadam'. Thanks to Tsongkhapa and other gifted scholars, such as Gyaltsab Darma Rinchen (1364–1432) and Khedrup Gelek Palzang (1385–1483), the Gelugpa tradition became renowned not only for its emphasis on monastic discipline but also for its specialisation in Pramana ('Valid Cognition'), teachings on logic and epistemology taught earlier in India by Dignaga and Dharmakirti and, in Tibet, by Chapa Chokyi Sengge (1109–1169) and Sakya Pandita (1182–1251). In addition to their scholarly repute, from 1649 until modern times, the Gelugpa enjoyed political power in Tibet through the office of the successive incarnations of the Dalai Lama, beginning with the fifth in the line, Ngawang Lozang Gyamtso (1617–1682). This hierarch of the monastery of Drepung had assumed the rule of Tibet with the support of his Mongol patrons at the conclusion of decades of religio-political struggles.

The Dakpo Kagyu School

The second of the major new tantric schools established in Tibet in the eleventh century was the Kagyu tradition originating with the translator Marpa from Lhodrak in southern Tibet. This latter obtained numerous anuttara tantra cycles such as Hevajra, Chakrasamvara and Vajravarahi while in India but, most importantly, from the siddhas Maitripa and Narotapa, he received the two cycles of instructions, known as The Great Seal (Skt. *mahamudra*; Tib. *chagya chenpo*) and 'The Six Doctrines'[8] which, over time, became the most celebrated Kagyupa teachings. Marpa's chief disciple was the yogin and poet Milarepa

(1040–1123), who in turn transmitted these instructions to the Kadampa monk Gampopa Sonam Rinchen (1079–1153). It was Gampopa, also known as Dakpo Lhaje, who, by blending together The Great Seal and the teachings of the Kadampa into one stream, endowed the Kagyu tradition both with its characteristic doctrinal and (largely monastic) institutional forms and its proper name 'Dakpo Kagyu'.

Following Gampopa, the Dakpo Kagyu tradition, transmitted through his four principal disciples, split into four major branches, the Phakmo Dru, the Tshal of Lama Zhang (1123–1194), the Baram of Baram Darma Wangchuk (1124–1197), and the Karma of Karmapa Dusum Khyenpa (1110–1193). The first of these, issuing from the great meditator Phakmo Dru Dorje Gyaltsen (1110–1170) engendered in its turn eight minor lines: Drukpa, Drigung, Taklung, Trophu, Yamzang, Shugse, Mar and Yel. In recent centuries the fourth major branch, the Karma Kagyu, led by the seventeen successive incarnations of H.H. Gyalwa Karmapa, embodiment of the bodhisattva Avalokiteshvara, has been the most wide-spread of the Kagyu schools and has now, under the guidance of H.H. Karmapa Thinley Thaye Dorje (b. 1983) and the late Shamar Rinpoche, Mipham Chokyi Lodro (1952–2014), spread throughout the entire world.

The Sakya School

The origins of the Sakya tradition are more or less contemporaneous with those of the Kagyu. Although its ruling dynasty, the Khon family, had links to the earlier period of dharma in Tibet, the history proper of the Sakya school began in 1073. In that year an illustrious member of the Khon family, Konchog Gyalpo, a disciple of Drokmi Lotsava, founded a dharma centre in Sakya, south-western Tibet, dedicated to the new tantras. The tradition, which thenceforth took its name from this first centre, was given definitive shape by Konchog Gyalpo's son, the 'Great Sakyapa', Kunga Nyingpo (1092–1158) who was heir, through his numerous teachers, to a vast range of sutra and tantra teachings, most importantly the siddha Virupa's *The Path and its Result* (Tib. *lam-dre*), which was based on the three tantras of Hevajra, and the siddha Narotapa's Vajrayogini practice cycle, which was derived from the Chakrasamvara tantra.

Sachen Kunga Nyingpo was followed in the lineage by two of his sons, Lopon Sonam Tsemo (1141–1182) and Jetsun Drakpa Gyaltsen (1147–1216), both of whose dual achievements in the fields of scholarship and tantric meditation endowed the burgeoning tradition with much of its distinctive ethos. The fourth of the great early masters of the tradition was Sakya Pandita Kunga Gyaltsen Pal Zangpo (1182–1251), renowned for his spiritual realisation and consummate mastery of both religious and secular fields of knowledge, acquired from his apprenticeship with his uncle Drakpa Gyaltsen and his studies with Shakyashribhadra and others from the final generation of Indian Buddhist scholars. During the lifetime of Chogyal Phakpa (1235–1281), nephew of Sakya Pandita and last of 'the five great masters', the reach and prestige of the Sakya tradition were further extended to Mongolia and parts of China when Kublai Khan became his disciple. At that time, the great Khan bestowed political authority over Tibet on his lama and, although their secular power waned in time, the Sakya tradition has continued to look to the Khon family as the dynastic heads of the tradition.

As numerous disciples of these five early masters taught throughout Tibet, the influence of the Sakya tradition upon Buddhism in Tibet became very extensive. Many significant masters from other schools received teachings from the holders of Sakya transmissions. Thus, in the course of time, the contribution made by the Sakyapas in the fields of scholarship and meditation shaped much of the pattern of dharma study and practice in all schools. Foremost among later Sakya scholars and practitioners were such celebrated thinkers as Gorampa Sonam Sengge and Shakya Chogden (1428–1507). More recently the famed Sakyapa master Jamyang Khyentse Wangpo (1820–1892) played a leading role in fostering the Rime ('non-sectarian') movement, which helped to bring about something of a renaissance of dharma in eastern Tibet.

In the course of time, two principal sub-sects of the Sakya tradition have arisen. The first is the Ngor sub-sect, founded by the great *Path and its Result* master Ngorchen Kunga Zangpo (1382–1457), which had its principal centre at Ngor in Tsang province. The second sub-sect is the Tsarpa, established by the Vajrayogini master Tsarchen Losal Gyamtso (1502–1556). The headquarters of the Tsar sub-sect was Nalendra monastery in Phenyul in Ü province.

From 1959 until 2017, when he stepped down from the position, the head of the Sakya tradition was H.H. Sakya Trizin, Ngawang Kunga Thegchen Palbar Samphel Wanggi Gyalpo, the forty-first holder of the throne of Sakya and emanation of the bodhisattva Manjushri. Born into the Dolma Palace branch of the Khon family in 1945, he has received extensive teachings from such masters as Ngawang Lodro Zhenphen Nyingpo, Jamyang Khyentse Chokyi Lodro and Chogye Trichen. In 1959, after the destruction of Tibetan independence, His Holiness, together with many of his followers, sought refuge in India where, at Dehra Dun in Uttar Pradesh, he has established his seat in exile. Under his guidance the Sakya tradition has been able to maintain itself in exile. His Holiness was succeeded as holder of the throne by his elder son, H.H. Ratna Vajra Rinpoche (b. 1974), who was in turn succeeded by his younger brother Gyana Vajra Rinpoche (b. 1979). Following that, the Sakya throne will be held for a certain period by members of the Phuntsok Palace branch of the Khon family.

Two
A Solid Rock

TAKING REFUGE

Reading the history of our predecessors in dharma might be inspiring, but to practise the dharma effectively we need to have confidence that, like them, we will be able to follow the path through to its end. In point of fact, the basis for such confidence already exists, in that our mind, whilst presently obscured by nescience and disturbing emotions, has never lost its primordial purity. Hence its capacity to manifest the wisdom and compassion of buddhahood is unspoiled. Thus there is every reason to enter the path—a path that begins with taking refuge.

To explain this in a little more detail: It is said in the sutras and tantras that mind itself, whether termed 'buddha-nature' or 'the all-base causal tantra', is the ground of both the suffering of cyclic existence and the bliss of enlightenment. Mind's essence is a union of clarity and emptiness, since it is a beginningless and unceasing stream of awareness, which, at the same time, is empty of any attributes by which it might be objectified. However, due to habitual patterns of confusion, its essence is obscured and this clear awareness is mistaken for something with the traits of substantial existence. Such a misreading acts as the stimulus for desire, the compulsion to grasp at the appearance of phenomena manifesting from mind's clarity as if they were real. Similarly, through the force of these imprints of confusion, mind's emptiness is mistaken for a bare non-existence, and such a misinterpretation acts as the stimulus for aggression, the compulsion to annihilate the variety of appearances.

This triad of the emotions of ignorance, desire and aggression prompts the actions (Skt. *karma*) that result in the diverse experiences and realms of cyclic existence (Skt. *samsara*), realms characterised by their pervasion by suffering. However, when one recognises and settles in the true nature of mind, which is none other than the union of clarity and emptiness, this chain of delusion, disturbing emotions, actions and consequent misery is brought to an end and one arrives at buddhahood, a state fully endowed with all enlightened qualities.

Although in such a manner the seed of buddhahood is present, since cyclic existence and its causes do not come to an end by themselves, one actually needs to enter the path which is the means to bring this about. One does so by the act of 'taking refuge', in which one entrusts oneself to the guidance represented by the objects of refuge—whether the three objects of refuge presented in the common vehicles or the four-fold refuge presented in the Vajrayana.

In going for refuge, one is seeking protection from the viciousness of cyclic existence, hence the use of the term 'refuge'. As Sakya Pandita says: 'It is termed refuge because it protects.'[9]

It is the act of taking refuge which signifies that one is a Buddhist (Tib. *sanjay-pa*) and that one's practice of hearing, reflecting and meditating constitutes a Buddhist path. Thus, after taking refuge for the first time in the presence of one's lama or a senior member of the sangha, one begins all sessions of practice with the refuge verses that one first recited in that ceremony.

The motivation for taking refuge

However, the mere performance of the ceremony of taking refuge and the continuing recitation of the refuge verses are of little benefit unless they are inspired and sustained by the appropriate motivation. Thus it is taught that one should go for refuge with a motivation that combines fear, confidence and compassion. In this context, 'fear' indicates one's wish to be protected by the objects of refuge from the suffering inherent in cyclic existence as was indicated above. In addition, for those who aspire to practise the Mahayana, it also signifies the fear of deviating into the lesser vehicle and thus abandoning the superior path. Finally, for Vajrayanists it signifies the fear of lapsing into impure vision.

Secondly, possessing the motivation of faith enables one to entrust oneself without hesitation to the support of the objects of refuge. As with fear, it too has three aspects: 'clear' faith is that inspired by the examples of Buddha or other representations of the qualities of enlightenment; secondly, 'longing' faith is that which wishes to acquire those qualities, and, finally, 'convinced' faith is the confidence deriving from one's reasoned conviction that the doctrine of actions, causes and results and the truths of the path and cessation of suffering are without error.

Thirdly, to take refuge with a compassionate motivation ensures that one possesses the altruistic intent that others also be protected by the objects of refuge.

Duration of taking refuge

The duration of taking refuge is correlated with the dharma path that one aspires to practise. In this respect, people who merely wish to avoid suffering while within samsara take refuge until they obtain some state of happiness in this or future lives. Shravakas and solitary realisers, with minds set on release from samsara, take refuge until they achieve their own individual liberation but not until supreme enlightenment, while Mahayanists, who wish to embark upon the bodhisattva career that culminates in supreme buddhahood, take refuge until the attainment of that state.

As Sakya Pandita says:

> Worldly people take refuge only until they attain some minor personal goal pertaining to this or the next life. Shravakas and solitary realisers, apart from stating 'as long as I shall live', do not maintain taking refuge until the stage of enlightenment is reached. Bodhisattvas take refuge until reaching the level of awakening.[10]

The objects in which one takes refuge

In the Shravakayana and Common Mahayana, the objects are three-fold, being the Buddha understood as one's teacher, the dharma as one's path and the sangha as one's companions on the path, but in the Vajrayana the objects are four in number, since the lama is also to be included. Here we will consider these objects of refuge individually:

The lama

In the Vajrayana, the lama is regarded an object of refuge because he or she is the very embodiment of the Three Jewels. As it is said:

> The lama is the Buddha
> The lama is the dharma
> The lama is the sangha also.
> He is the activity of all.[11]

By contrast with this Vajrayana perspective, in the common systems the master is not viewed as an object of refuge. However, he does play an important and necessary role therein, as Nagarjuna makes clear in *The Friendly Letter:*

> Since the Sage has taught that reliance on a spiritual friend
> Completely perfects the pure conduct
> One should rely upon holy beings.[12]

In these common systems, the teacher's role is analogous to that of a guide, an escort or a ferryman who could respectively lead, guard and carry one forward on the path. Specifically, in the Shravakayana, the master's most important function is to impart the moral discipline of that system and in the Common Mahayana or, as it is sometimes termed, 'The Vehicle of the Perfections', it is to bestow the bodhisattva vow.

Regarding the significant differences in how the lama is to be regarded in the three vehicles, Sakya Pandita states:

> However good he may be
> A teacher of the Shravaka system is simply an ordinary person
> While one of the Perfections system
> Is, if good, the jewel of the sangha.
> However, an excellent master of the Mantra system
> Is none other than the Three Jewels.[13]

And again:

> While the scriptural tradition of the Perfections
> States that a lama should be regarded as 'like a buddha'
> It does not claim that he is actually a buddha.
> The lama who is actually a buddha
> Is the one from whom initiation is received.[14]

The principal teachings bestowed by the Vajrayana master are three-fold: initiations, textual transmissions and guiding instructions, and chief among these three functions is the bestowal of initiation. Since it is only by receiving these that we are permitted to embark upon Vajrayana practice, one should examine the master as to whether he does indeed possess the requisite qualities and qualifications that fit him to carry out such duties. Concerning these qualifications, *The Fifty Verses on the Guru* declares:

> He should be skilled in the method of the mantras and tantras, full of loving compassion and learned in the scriptures.[15]

In addition, a Vajrayana teacher will only perform his tasks with the permission of his own masters. Again as it is said in *The Fifty Verses*:

> Without the permission of your master, do not perform consecrations, mandalas or fire-offerings, do not gather disciples and do not teach.[16]

Having found such a Vajrayana master, one should hear, reflect and then meditate upon his instructions. Through this process, what begins as sincere respect and appreciation will flower as authentic devotion towards him. In the end, one realises that, since the Vajrayana master leads us to buddhahood through his ripening initiations and liberating instructions, it is appropriate and skilful to view him as consubstantial with the particular buddha whose initiation he has bestowed.

The Buddha

The jewel of Buddha is the first of the Three Jewels (Tib. *konchog sum*, i.e. 'The Three Rare and Excellent Ones'), since the succeeding two jewels are entirely dependent upon him. This dependency follows from the fact that it was the Buddha who revealed the jewel of the dharma and the jewel of the sangha itself consists of those who follow the path of dharma thus elucidated by the Buddha.

Referring to Buddha's primacy among the Three Jewels, Maitreya declared in *The Supreme Continuum Treatise*:

> In the ultimate sense, only the Buddha is the refuge of beings, because the Conqueror possesses the body of the dharma (dharmakaya) and this is the ultimate attainment of the sangha.[17]

A buddha, as exemplified by the historical Shakyamuni, is someone who, having generated bodhichitta and thus determined on the attainment of buddhahood for the benefit of all beings, gathers the two accumulations of merit and wisdom by practising the six perfections, the transcendental virtues of giving, moral discipline, patience, effort, meditation and wisdom or, described most essentially, by developing immeasurable compassion and wisdom. By so doing, he purifies the obscurations of disturbing emotions and nescience and finally awakens to the actual unelaborated nature of all phenomena, which awakening constitutes the bliss of buddhahood.

As Sonam Tsemo says:

> If one asks what are the characteristics of a buddha, they are three in number: the unmistaken realisation of the true nature of reality, the possession of stainless bliss and the abandonment of all obscurations without exception.[18]

Furthermore, as we noted in the previous chapter, a buddha possesses different modes of being. Expressed simply, they are two-fold: the dharmakaya ('the truth body') and rupakaya ('the form body'). The first of these, the dharmakaya, flows from his acquisition of the knowledge of the true nature of reality, a wisdom which every buddha has attained. As the true nature of reality itself, the object of this knowledge, is free from arising or cessation and is ungraspable by concept or designation, so the dharmakaya, the state of knowing this, is unproduced, unceasing and unelaborated.

Since the dharmakaya, the ultimate reality of all buddhas, is thus by its very nature inaccessible to the dualistic perception of unenlightened beings, the Buddha, in order to show them the way to liberation from suffering, manifests to such beings as the rupakaya, the effortless expression of his unrestricted compassion. Such a mode of manifestation can be likened to the way in which, while the moon remains in the sky, its image is reflected in countless pools of water upon the earth. In this analogy, the Buddha's dharmakaya is represented by the moon and the Buddha's rupakaya by the moon's reflections, while the innumerable pools represent the minds of those to be taught.

In actuality, the rupakaya itself possesses two modes of appearance related to the two different levels on which the beings to be trained actually dwell. Thus, in the realms of splendour attained by spiritually advanced bodhisattvas, the Buddha displays the sambhogakaya ('enjoyment body') form endowed with 'the five certainties' of teacher, time, place, audience, and teaching.[19] However, for ordinary beings in mundane realms such as ours, the Buddha manifests a variety of nirmanakaya ('emanation body') forms to present the dharma, as we briefly touched upon in the previous chapter. These nirmanakaya forms are divided into three distinct types: a nirmanakaya of birth, which the Buddha manifests in such roles as that of a monarch or even in non-human forms in order to benefit beings; a nirmanakaya of skill, whereby he trains beings through such devices as artistic performance; and a supreme nirmanakaya, through which a buddha reveals himself openly as a buddha and accomplishes the twelve great deeds to lead beings to enlightenment.

Since in the true nature of reality attained by buddhas there is neither singularity nor multiplicity, a fourth kaya of the Buddha is often designated—the svabhavikakaya ('the essence body') to indicate that the preceding three kayas possess an intrinsic unity.

Taking refuge in the Buddha, who embodies these qualities and modes of being, is of extraordinary importance, since the jewel of Buddha represents the fulfilment of one's own innate potential for buddhahood. Thus, through taking refuge in this jewel, one has formed a connection to the reality of enlightenment.

The dharma

The path to buddhahood taught by Lord Buddha is presented in the jewel of the dharma. This jewel is two-fold: the dharma of direct realisation and the dharma of scriptural tradition. 'Direct realisation' is the experiential insight into the true nature of reality expressed in the third and fourth noble truths proclaimed by the Buddha—the experience of the truth of the path and the consequent experience of the truth of cessation of suffering. However, although this realisation itself is the crucial event in one's spiritual life, its occurrence depends upon the systematic study and practice of the teachings contained in the scriptural tradition, the other aspect of the jewel of dharma, for it is this which provides the foundation from which such experiential insight springs.

The dharma of scriptural tradition is expressed in the words of the Buddha collected in the three 'baskets' of sutra, abhidharma,[20] and vinaya.[21] Some masters maintain that these teachings were given by Lord Buddha in three distinct periods, known as 'the three turnings of the wheel', in which he presented the doctrine at differing levels of subtlety. Thus in the first period, or 'first turning of the wheel of dharma', Lord Buddha explained the doctrines of the Shravakayana, such as the four noble truths, comprising the truths of suffering and its cause—self-clinging, and the cessation of suffering and its cause—the path. In the second period he discoursed on the Mahayana topics such as the *Perfection of Wisdom* with its emphasis on the lack of abiding essence in any phenomena and in the third or final period he gave teachings on further Mahayana doctrines such as 'Mind Only' and buddha-nature. However, other masters, such as Lopon Sonam Tsemo, assert that, while such doctrines were indeed taught, they were taught in one single transmission but the Buddha and his teachings were visualised and heard in these three different ways according to the aptitudes present within the audience, and it is this last fact which is reflected in the terminology of 'the three turnings of the wheel'.

Thus Sonam Tsemo declares:

An inconceivable variety of teachings were expressed for different trainees, yet at a single time and in a single place, proclaimed with different arrangements of bodies and speech as an inexpressible number of sutras and tantras.[22]

As indicated in the first chapter, and as mentioned above in passing by Sonam Tsemo, in addition to these 'sutra' teachings, the 'buddha-word' also includes the 'mantra' teachings of Vajrayana. These esoteric instructions, having been first proclaimed in 'the pure realms' were collected by the bodhisattva Vajrapani, 'Lord of Secrets', and preserved in the scriptural redactions known as 'tantras' before being transmitted in this world.

The sangha

Just as the jewel of the dharma announced by the Buddha constitutes the path to enlightenment, so the jewel of the sangha constitutes the companions who help us to travel that path. The sangha itself is two-fold—the 'noble sangha' consisting of those who have attained irreversible levels of the path[23] and the 'ordinary sangha' of practitioners who have entered the dharma prior to us.

The arhats[24] and bodhisattvas[25] who comprise the noble sangha include such figures as Lord Buddha's renunciate disciples Shariputra and Mahamaudgalyayana, who obtained arhatship, and lay bodhisattvas, such as Manjushri and Avalokiteshvara, who scaled the ten Mahayana noble spiritual levels.[26] In the Vajrayana, the noble sangha is formed by those practitioners who have achieved transcendental levels of realisation, parallel to those in the general Mahayana, through the methods of the tantric system and who are thus known as 'siddhas' ('accomplished ones'). The example of their perfect conduct and the power of their meditation remain as a source of blessings for subsequent generations of practitioners.

The sangha of ordinary practitioners denotes practitioners of each of the three vehicles. Thus the sangha of the Shravakayana is comprised of those who uphold the pratimoksha ('individual liberation') vows as fully-ordained renunciates. Those, whether monastic or lay, who uphold the bodhisattva vow to achieve buddhahood for the benefit of all beings comprise the ordinary Mahayana sangha, and those who maintain the vidyadhara vows,[27] received at the time of tantric initiation, are known as the Vajrayana sangha. Since the vidyadhara vow includes the pratimoksha and bodhisattva vow, the Vajrayana sangha can be considered holders of all three vows.

Thus, on taking refuge in the sangha, one enters into a fellowship which is resolved upon the practice of the dharma. One's own commitment to the path is consequently located in the wider environment of collective practice, a fact which helps in overcoming the difficulties that inevitably occur in the spiritual life.

While the lama, Buddha, dharma and sangha are to be regarded as the four-fold Vajrayana refuge, many Kagyu and Nyingma sources[28] describe each of the Three Jewels as having a corresponding Vajrayana object of refuge. These are known collectively as 'the three roots'. Thus the tantric aspect of Buddha is the lama, who is the 'root' of the blessings that ripen one's mind, the essential function of a Vajrayana master. The tantric aspect of the dharma is the yidam (meditation deity), root of accomplishments (Skt. *siddhi*), since these are the fruit of such deity meditation. Finally, the tantric aspect of the sangha is represented by the dakini (Tib. *khandroma,* literally 'sky-goer'), who comprises the root of activities that guard the progress of the practitioner.

The method of taking refuge

According to Konchog Lhundrup, one should:

> Hold the mind in one-pointed devotion to one's lamas and the Buddha as the illuminators who show one the path to complete liberation; to the dharma as the actual path itself and to the sangha as one's helpers who assist one in completing that path.[29]

As the actual verse of refuge, one could recite:

> I take refuge in the lama
> I take refuge in the Buddha
> I take refuge in the dharma
> I take refuge in the sangha.

After taking refuge, if one so wishes, one can request the bestowal of the pratimoksha vow, which represents the discipline of the Shravaka system. The monastic or 'renunciate' form of this discipline, which can only be acquired from the requisite members of the monastic sangha, comprises numerous vows, most importantly the four root vows of abstention from taking human life, sexual intercourse, theft and lies concerning spiritual status. However, for lay practitioners, the discipline, which does not require a monastic quorum for its transmission, consists, in its fullest form, of the five trainings of abstaining from: taking life, theft, sexual misconduct, false and harmful speech and intoxication. As regards this vow, even without formally committing to any particular number of these precepts, one can maintain an 'essential' form of the discipline by committing oneself to refrain from activities which harm others.[30]

The adoption of such ethical guidelines creates the space in which one can apply oneself to meditation, free from the turbulence caused by indulgent behaviour. Furthermore, these precepts will subsequently serve as a stepping-stone towards the altruism that is expressed in the bodhisattva vow of the Mahayana.

Milarepa

THREE
Tasting Birth and Death

THE FOUR THOUGHTS THAT TURN THE MIND

Having taken refuge, one's life has a firm foundation, a basis for travelling the path without being blown off course. However, to preserve and extend this new stability a decisive break with one's worldly habits and values is required. This comes about through systematic reflection on the 'four thoughts'—precious human birth, impermanence, action, causes and results, and, fourthly, the defects of samsara ('cyclic existence').

This series of contemplations serve as a common entry-point for the three vehicles, since the possibility of making progress on the paths to liberation and buddhahood depends upon the change in our attitudes brought about by these fundamental teachings. By stripping bare the reality of our present entanglement in the cycle of birth and death, they cause us to seek liberation.

These preliminary teachings have been set forth in various contexts. Thus, in the system known as *The Graduated Path of the Three Persons* elaborated originally by Atisha, the 'four thoughts' function as the contemplations to be utilised by the first two types of practitioner—the 'inferior' and 'mediocre' persons. In the Sakya texts on *Parting from the Four Attachments*, they are considered to be the remedy for the first two attachments—'attachment to this life' and 'attachment to the three worlds (of cyclic existence)'—while, in some presentations of *The Path and its Result*, they are taught as the remedial contemplations for those afflicted by the 'impure vision'. Finally, in the Kagyu and Nyingma traditions, the four thoughts function as the 'common preliminaries' for the practices of mahamudra and dzok chen respectively.

As regards the order in which one should contemplate them, here the sequence as presented by Gorampa Sonam Sengge in his *Key to the Profound Meaning*[31] has been followed. Nevertheless, having contemplated them in this order, one could vary the sequence as one wishes, since employing different perspectives in that way can bring out a more profound sense of this teaching.

PRECIOUS HUMAN BIRTH

For this first contemplation, one should consider both the advantages and the rarity of human birth, the two factors comprising its preciousness.

Its Advantages

Having a human birth provides the supportive conditions for liberation. As we have already considered, all sentient beings in the six realms of existence possess the buddha-nature, the seed of buddhahood. However, only those who have obtained human birth are in a position to bring this seed to fruition, since it is human life that affords us the necessary degree of freedom to determine our destinies and, at the same time, it embodies exactly the mix of suffering and happiness that can galvanise us to enter the path.

As Konchog Lhundrup states:

> If one obtains this body, it is more precious than a
> wish-fulfilling jewel.[32]

And again:

> This human body endowed with the prerequisites
> is more suitable for dharma-practice than any from
> the other realms.[33]

Its Rarity

However, although so beneficial, human birth is difficult
to obtain in the cycle of birth and death. That rarity can
be considered in regard to human birth's causal roots, its
numerical rarity and its actual essence.

Its chief cause is prior virtuous—one might say
'humane'—behaviour. To understand this point, one needs
to remember that causes and effects must always be related
and not of an utterly dissimilar nature, as is confirmed by
the valid reasoning related to dependent origination. Since
the putative causes of human birth, virtuous actions, are
far outnumbered, even among those who are currently
humans, by non-virtuous actions, the result, human birth
itself, can only occur relatively infrequently. Indeed, a
human life in which a strong inclination to goodness and
dharma is present and which therefore truly merits the
name 'precious human birth', is even more rare.

In addition, compared to birth into other forms of
sentient life in this infinite universe, birth into a human
life is numerically infinitesimal, and, having been born in
other forms of life, it requires the ripening of deeds from
past lives, in which one did practise virtue, as the impelling
and culminating force to propel one into a favourable
human birth. That such circumstances are extremely

infrequent is underlined by Shantideva in *Entering the Bodhisattva Conduct*:

> The Lord therefore said that it is as difficult to obtain human birth as it is for a turtle's neck to enter a hole in a yoke floating on the ocean.[34]

As to its essence—what renders precious human birth a uniquely suitable basis for attaining buddhahood is its freedom from eight limitations and its possession of ten positive factors. It is precisely these that allow us to define such a life as a 'precious human life'.

These eight limitations that preclude the possibility of engaging in dharma practice are:

Birth as a hell being
Birth as a ghost
Birth as a god
Birth as an animal
Birth as a person lacking intact senses
Birth in a culture lacking a moral sensibility
Possessing tenacious wrong views
Living at a time in which no buddha has appeared.

The ten positive conditions that facilitate a relationship with the dharma are:

Birth as a human being
Dwelling in a land where the dharma is present
Possessing sound senses
Possessing faith in the dharma
Having refrained from the five 'heinous actions'[35]
A buddha has appeared
A buddha has taught the dharma
The dharma still exists
The dharma has genuine followers

There are others who have compassion and support
one's practice.

Having obtained such a human birth endowed with these
eight freedoms and ten positive factors, it would be an act
of folly to squander it. As it says in *The Friendly Letter*:

Having obtained a human birth,
one who commits sins
is more foolish than
one who fills a jewel-adorned golden vessel with vomit.[36]

IMPERMANENCE AND DEATH

At this point in contemplation, our sense of the value of
this life needs to be enhanced by the recognition of its
impermanence, lest we be made complacent by our present
good fortune and delay our engagement with the dharma.
To bring about the necessary sense of urgency, there is no
greater stimulus than the contemplation of impermanence.

In actuality, impermanence runs through every aspect
of our experience, since all conditioned phenomena are,
by their very nature of arising from causes and conditions,
utterly transient. Thus, as is commonly said:

The end of all meeting is parting.
The end of all gathering is dispersal.
The end of all rising is falling.
The end of all birth is death.

And, as Mipham Rinpoche states:

Understand that all conditioned phenomena
are impermanent, because they arise and cease
moment by moment.[37]

Such is the general meaning of impermanence. However, to cast off the obstacles to dharma-practice caused by laziness in its various forms, it is especially useful to meditate upon three particular themes—the certainty of death, the uncertainty of the time of its occurrence and the uselessness of anything other than the dharma at that time.

1. Contemplating the certainty of death in three points:

A. One should consider that there is not a single example of anyone in history who has escaped death. How could we think that somehow we would be spared this fate? As it says in *Entering the Bodhisattva Conduct*:

> Why should it not be that death should befall such a
> one as me?[38]

B. As we have already noted, decay and collapse are woven into the very fabric of the universe. Thus it is inevitable that this temporary union of body and mind, which union actually constitutes my present life, will come to an end. As it is said in *The Thirty-Seven Practices of a Buddha's Child*:

> The mind is just a guest in the hotel of the body.
> One day it must depart and travel beyond.[39]

C. Every day brings us closer to that inevitable end. Death is never receding or even standing still. In fact, our situation resembles that of a prisoner condemned to death—with every day his execution draws closer.

If, at this juncture, we are prepared to concede the inevitability of death but still want to put off engagement with the dharma until some later date, we should utilise the next contemplation.

2. Contemplating the uncertainty of the time of death in three points:

A. There is no fixed span of life among humans.

As it is said:

> Some die while in the womb;
> So, too, some die on just being born;
> So, too, some die while just crawling;
> Some, too, while able to run about;
> Some old and some young;
> Some while in the prime of life.[40]

B. Many dangers surround us—whether it is disorder in the natural elements that make up our body and the environment or whether it is dangers that have been artificially created.

As Nagarjuna says:

> There are so many dangers besetting our life.
> If it is no more permanent
> Than a bubble of water blown by the wind,
> Why should exhalation follow inhalation
> Or waking follow sleeping?
> It is a great wonder.[41]

C. By contrast with forces that threaten life, there are relatively few that protect it. Indeed, even supportive systems like food, scientific work or medical treatment can be fatal in certain situations. Thus the reality of death is always with us.

3. Contemplating that, at the time of death, nothing other than dharma will be useful:

At the moment of death, mind and body separate and go their own different ways. Those things upon which we have placed so much reliance—our friends and relations, the wealth that we have accumulated and our power and intellect—will not help us. Only prior practice of the dharma will be of any use for our mind's journey into the intermediate state and the next life.

ACTIONS, CAUSES AND RESULTS

This last contemplation should lead us to the consideration that, at death, nothing other than the imprints of our actions, virtuous or non-virtuous, will accompany our mind.

As it says in *The Sutra of Advice to the King*:

When the time comes to depart, O king,
Neither possessions, friends nor relatives can follow.
However, wherever beings come from, wherever they go,
Their actions follow them like a shadow.[42]

In actuality, the whole range of life-situations that comprise samsara have their roots in our actions (Skt. *karma*). No external power, nor random chance, have contrived our present position in the cycle of birth and death. The imprints of our actions—physical, verbal and mental—are deposited in the basic continuum of our mind and ripen, when the appropriate conditions obtain, as the various sufferings and joys of life in the six realms. Since mind itself, being non-physical, cannot be destroyed and therefore continues to be embodied in a variety of forms and environments until liberation, there is no limit to the ripening of deeds prior to buddhahood.

At this point it is crucial to understand the nature of actions and the means of distinguishing virtuous actions from those of non-virtue.

As for the nature of actions themselves, it says in the Abhidharma:

What are actions? They are intention and what results from intention in speech and body.[43]

As regards their virtuous or non-virtuous nature, Nagarjuna declares:

Actions arising from desire, hatred and ignorance are non-virtues.
Actions arising from the freedom from desire, hatred and ignorance are virtues.[44]

Actions springing from the three 'poisons' just delineated have their fundamental origin in attachment to self, since wherever such an attitude is present, there is a division between self and other—a rupture which underpins all disturbing emotions. Thus the mark of an authentically moral life is not the mere observation of correct external behaviour but the development of a wisdom that aligns us with the true nature of reality, in which the delusion of selfhood is extinguished. Nonetheless, although we do not yet possess such definitive understanding of reality, we should adopt virtuous behaviour now as it will be a basis, not only for future happiness within the succession of lives, but also for the development of that wisdom.

Incidentally, one should be careful not to confuse the insistence that motivation is a major determinant of the moral character of any action with the sentimental assumption that unexamined 'good intentions' are sufficient to render a particular action virtuous. In this respect, one should remember that ignorance, defined in dharma as the refusal to acknowledge the link between causes and effects, is itself non-virtuous. Hence, precisely since an important part of the moral character of an action stems from the effect it has on others and oneself, one must abandon the wilful ignorance demonstrated in naive and deceptive appeals to mere 'good intention' and strive to investigate the potential consequences of actions.

Similarly, any claims that we do not need to be concerned with virtue and non-virtue since dharma is 'beyond good and evil' demonstrate the erroneous belief aptly characterised by Padmakara as 'the view of empty of sin—empty of virtue'.[45] In a similar vein, notions that we can disregard the very specific ethical injunctions of the Buddha, 'that most skilful of physicians', and replace them by contemporary nostrums are equally mistaken.

Contemplating non-virtues and their results

There are ten primary non-virtuous actions:

> Taking life[46]
> Taking what is not given
> Sexual misconduct
> Lying
> Slander
> Harsh speech
> Frivolous speech
> Covetousness
> Malevolence
> Wrong views.

These sinful actions mature as sufferings in various ways. In general, it can be said that deeds motivated by aggression lead to birth in the hell realm, those motivated by avarice to birth in the ghost realm, and those motivated by ignorance to birth in the animal realm. Moreover, the fruit of deeds can ripen in 'experiences similar to the causes', an example of which would be the manner in which killing can generate a vulnerability to early death. The force of actions can also mature in the establishment of habits, characterised as 'results maturing as actions similar to the cause'. An instance of this would be the brutalisation that can develop once the act of killing has been performed, a coarsening which makes it more likely that we will kill again. In such a manner, one sees how the repeated practice of non-virtue shrinks our capacity for goodness. One's actions can also influence one's future physical and social environment. An example of this process would be the manner in which the action of killing may ripen as rebirth into an environment where the necessities for supporting life are scarce.

Before leaving this topic of non-virtue, one should note that, although the ripening of actions is said to be inevitable, negative deeds can be purified by an act of confession embodying 'the four powers'—of regretting one's non-virtue, committing to desist from such actions henceforth, having confidence that this confession is an effective antidote and relying on the sustaining goodness represented by the buddhas. If one were to combine these four powers with the recitation of *The Three Heaps Sutra* ('*Confession before the Thirty-Five Buddhas*') or the meditations upon Vajrasattva or Samayavajra, one's confession would be especially effective.

Contemplating virtuous actions and their results

The ten virtuous actions may simply be described as the abandoning of the ten sinful deeds. Thus, for example, the renunciation of killing constitutes the primary virtuous deed. Just as negative actions produce the miseries of samsara, so all the joyful experiences encountered in the six realms originate in one's virtuous deeds. Since this is so, one should delight in such actions.

Contemplating neutral deeds

Neutral deeds are those which do not arise from either a virtuous or non-virtuous intention and therefore do not generate any karmic result. This category of deeds includes activities such as walking, sitting and sleeping and also arts and crafts.

One can strive to convert such actions into virtue by applying skilful means with mindfulness and clear comprehension—for instance, one might dedicate the action to the benefit of others with the thought: 'May this action produce the welfare of others'.

To keep these instructions on actions, causes and results in mind, it is very helpful to recall the words of Patrul Rinpoche:

> To see your previous births, look at what you are now. To see where you are going to be born next, look at what you do now.[47]

DEFECTS OF SAMSARA

The fourth and final reflection is the contemplation of worldly existence and its sufferings, contrived, as they are, by our actions, as we have just understood. This suffering displays itself in three modes: the suffering of suffering; the suffering of change; and the suffering of conditionality.

1. The suffering of suffering is constituted by rebirth in the three lower realms—those of animals, ghosts and hell-beings—situations where misery is relatively undisguised and where the only happiness to be found is in their passing.

As Jetsun Drakpa Gyaltsen says:

> The suffering of suffering is the misery of the three lower realms.[48]

The causes of existence in these lower realms lie within our own mind. If, at the time of death, aggression is dominant in our mental continuum, the imprint of this defilement will ripen as rebirth into a variety of hellish environments until the force of our past aggression is exhausted and can no longer ripen as such projections. Likewise, the experience of rebirth into the ghost realm is structured through the imprints of avarice, causing one to experience a series of hallucinatory episodes of deprivation.

Finally, rebirth in the animal realm comes about through the defilement of ignorance: the habitual disuse of one's capacity for reflection and choice, themselves the seeds of virtuous action. In this realm, as is often sadly evident, animals endure a life of being preyed upon and of preying upon their fellows, and of helpless slavery and exploitation.

2. The suffering of change obtains in the three higher realms and is displayed in the manner in which every situation that appears to promise lasting happiness, success, wealth or power, inevitably reveals itself as suffering in a new guise, when the object of happiness departs. Thus, in considering the human realm, one cannot deny that, despite fleeting moments of bliss, one is bound by the four rivers of birth, old age, sickness and death. Furthermore, in human life, one is also afflicted by the desire for what one cannot have, the difficulty of maintaining what one has, the pain of separation from one's dear ones, and association with hateful people.

Both the demi-god (Skt. *asura*) and god (Skt. *deva*) hallucinatory realms are also irredeemably flawed. In this regard, the pleasures of the god realm, deriving as they do from a mixture of virtue and pride, may seem, at first glance, to represent a life of permanent bliss but their built-in flaw is their very transitoriness. In addition, in the case of those reborn in the realm of the demi-gods, a further suffering inherent in their experience is their continuing frustrated struggle for spiritual power or status, a struggle deriving from jealousy. Thus one should not be trapped by the limited aim of gaining the pleasures of the higher realms, whether as a human or divine being. These environments, however seemingly wondrous, are no refuge from samsara, simply other facets of it.

3. The suffering of conditionality is the most fundamental of sufferings, for it inheres in one's mistaken notion that one's five aggregates of form, feeling, perception, formations and consciousness—the totality of conditioned phenomena—constitute, either singly or collectively, an autonomous, singular, permanent identity. This delusion acts as a magnet, attracting to itself all miseries from life to life. However, ordinary beings do not recognise this fabrication of the 'I' or 'self' out of the aggregates as suffering, but instead believe it to be the source of happiness. Only those who possess the eye of insight see this suffering of conditionality for what it is:

> A single hair on the palm of the hand,
> If it enters the eye,
> Causes unpleasantness and pain.
> The fools who resemble the palm of the hand
> Do not feel the hair, the suffering of conditionality,
> But saintly people, who are like the eye,
> Realise its nature as suffering.[49]

Contemplating such defects of samsara produces a longing for freedom and this, in turn, generates an unshakeable commitment to dharma-practice, since it is only this that can win us liberation from the cycle of birth and death.

Sonam Tsemo

Four
Open Heart

Love, Compassion and Bodhichitta

One should understand that, although the sense of renunciation engendered by 'the four thoughts' is crucial for authentic engagement with the path, it is insufficient for buddhahood. Just as a tree must be cut from the root, likewise, for samsara to be brought to an end, its root or primary cause, clinging to the notion of self, must be excised. Furthermore, the only means of bringing this about is bodhichitta, and, for this excision to be fully effective, one must develop bodhichitta in both of its forms—conventional bodhichitta arising from compassion and ultimate bodhichitta arising from wisdom—the first restraining self-clinging and the second entirely removing it.

As Konchog Lhundrup states:

Through meditation upon them, conventional bodhichitta restrains self-clinging and ultimate bodhichitta is then able to extract self-clinging from the root.[50]

Therefore, firstly, one should strive to develop conventional bodhichitta, so termed because this altruistic attitude is necessarily developed with a 'conventional' or 'relative' perspective.

To define and distinguish these two perspectives, Sakya Pandita has explained:

> 'Conventional truths' designate that which is perceived as existent in a non-analytic cognition and 'ultimate truth' refers to the non-finding of any existent phenomenon in an analytic cognition'.[51]

Hence, in developing conventional bodhichitta, one operates with an outlook that accepts the appearances of 'self' and 'other' and 'suffering' and 'liberation from suffering' without any examination as to their actual reality. However, if one were to analyse these appearances as to their actual mode of existence, one would discover that ultimately they are empty of any intrinsic nature, due to their being merely dependently arising phenomena. Nevertheless, here one utilises the 'conventional' perspective initially, since until the wisdom that recognises intrinsic emptiness arises, one will inevitably continue to think in terms of 'self' and 'other' and this perspective, at least, gives a sufficient basis for the development of compassion.

Thus conventional bodhichitta serves as the entrance-door to ultimate bodhichitta, and its own catalyst is the understanding that, since neither oneself nor others exist as totally discrete beings unconnected with one another, any intention to untie oneself alone from this net of suffering, in which all are imprisoned, is mistaken. Instead one must open one's heart to the world now in the resolve to attain buddhahood for the benefit of all beings. As it says in *Parting from the Four Attachments*:

There is no benefit in liberating oneself alone, for
the beings of the three realms are my fathers and
mothers. To leave my parents in the midst of distress,
while desiring happiness, would be evil-hearted.[52]

With the arising of such bodhichitta, one enters into the
practice of the second of the three vehicles, the Mahayana.
As Sakya Pandita says:

In the system of the Perfections of the Mahayana
there is no other dharma than bodhichitta.[53]

In fact, even the liberation for which one might wish in
following the Shravakayana is itself unattainable without
bodhichitta. The habitual unawareness which imprisons
us within samsara can only be transcended through
bodhichitta, the awakened thought which transforms the
ignorant attitudes of self-cherishing and self-clinging into
all-embracing compassion and wisdom. Once such a kind
of alchemy is at work, it provides the continuing impetus
to buddhahood. As it is said in *Entering the Bodhisattva
Conduct*:

It is like the supreme gold-making elixir,
For it transforms the unclean body we have taken
Into the precious jewel of a Buddha-form.
Therefore firmly seize the bodhichitta.[54]

The bodhisattva vow

This bodhichitta resolution itself is embodied in the
ceremony of the bodhisattva vow, through which one
formally enters into the Mahayana, just as through the
ceremony of refuge one formally becomes a Buddhist.
Incidentally, if one wonders whether there is also a
ceremony for the generation of ultimate bodhichitta, one

should understand that ultimate bodhichitta is the non-dual insight into the unelaborated nature of reality and thus, unlike conventional bodhichitta, it cannot arise from a ritual which is, unavoidably, contrived from words and gestures.

As Sakya Pandita explains:

> The generation of ultimate bodhichitta is not dependent on what the master recites. By the power of pleasing the buddhas and gathering vast accumulations of merit and wisdom after the highest worldly experience, there will arise the path of vision, the non-conceptual transcendental wisdom regarding phenomena. This is known as the generation of ultimate bodhichitta, since, unlike the generation of conventional bodhichitta, it does not rely upon a ritual for its generation.[55]

Nevertheless the ritual of the bodhisattva vow is an appropriate skilful means both for prompting the arising of conventional bodhichitta and for ensuring the ongoing maintenance of this commitment.

There are four main lineages through which the bodhisattva vow has been transmitted, each with its own distinct ritual and disciplines. Thus, in the Common Mahayana, the Vehicle of the Perfections, there are the two transmissions belonging to the Chittamatra and Madhyamaka tenet-systems. One can learn their distinctive characteristics and method elsewhere. In the Uncommon Mahayana, the Vajrayana, the bodhisattva vow is invariably transmitted in the preliminary part of any initiation. In addition, there is a special transmission of the bodhisattva vow given during the bestowal of *The Path and its Result* teachings in the Sakya tradition.

Once we have taken the bodhisattva vow, we should repeat our commitment each day as part of our preliminaries, alongside the verses of taking refuge. In fact, one could employ the combined verse of taking refuge and generating bodhichitta composed by Atisha:

> To the Buddha, dharma and supreme assembly
> I go for refuge until the heart of enlightenment.
> By the merit of giving and so forth
> May I attain Buddhahood for all beings.

Limitless Loving-Kindness

To practise the stages of meditation which culminate in bodhichitta, one should employ the Kadam instructions known as 'the seven-fold sequence of cause and effect', in which the meditations on the two 'limitlesses'—loving-kindness and compassion— comprise the preliminary stage, while meditation on bodhichitta forms the main stage of practice. Incidentally, in this context the term 'limitless' signifies that love and compassion are to be extended to all beings without exception, to endure without end, and that the merit thus produced is likewise immeasurable.

In this system, the key to engendering loving-kindness and compassion is the perception of all beings as our kin. To develop such a perception, one should begin with the following consideration: if one were to search for a first moment of samsara and of the minds of sentient beings, one could not find any such initial moment, since it would itself have to depend upon a prior moment out of which it arose, just as every effect depends for its manifestation upon prior causes and conditions.

As Chogyal Phakpa explains:

> A mind has no other cause than the mind itself. Though momentary, it is not without cause. Mind itself is the cause of mind, and mind is therefore free from the extreme of beginning.[56]

The consequence of this is that an infinite amount of time has already passed, thus providing the space in which all sentient beings have been directly related to one another innumerable times.

As Nagarjuna says:

> If one could count one's mothers with beads the
>   size of juniper seeds,
> They would cover more space than the entire earth.[57]

With the establishment of this perspective, one can proceed to practise loving-kindness meditation, taking one's own present mother as the initial object of meditation. Recollecting her many acts of kindness inspires an acknowledgement of one's indebtedness to her, a debt which can only be repaid through generating the wish, resolution and prayer that she might obtain happiness and the causes of future happiness, causes which consist in her developing moral behaviour from this time forward. As this meditative intention towards one's mother becomes resolute, one should extend it gradually towards one's other relatives, friends, enemies, and, eventually, to the whole of the six realms, in the understanding that, although one might not recognise them now and may even feel indifference or hostility towards them, nevertheless each and every being has been one's mother. Therefore each of them is connected with oneself just as intimately as the mother of this life, and, as such, they cannot be excluded from one's benevolence. The effect of this is that the intensity of affection towards this present mother is expanded to encompass all beings.

LIMITLESS COMPASSION

Once loving-kindness has become a stable feature in our outlook, one can proceed to meditation on compassion, which is the wish that all beings be liberated from suffering and its causes, which are sinful actions. It is to be cultivated in the same stages of meditation as the preceding meditation, beginning with our present mother and reaching fulfilment in the pervasion of all beings with a steady, undiminishing intention.

A particular point which is worthy of attention here concerns the attachment that people generally feel towards loved ones. If one utilises this attachment skilfully, it will not be an obstacle but an aid to the development of open-heartedness. One's love for one's children or parents, for instance, works in this meditation like a magnet to attract to itself all other beings, since they too are our parents and children, albeit from other times and other places. It would be a sad error to imagine that, before embracing all beings with tenderness, one had first to coldly reject those who are at this time our closest companions and dependants. How could universal love grow from such stony ground?

BODHICHITTA

Acknowledging our kinship with others creates a penetrating sense of their suffering. Yet, how can our wish that they might have happiness and be free from sorrow be achieved? At this very moment, they may be floundering in an ocean of misery, but, in our present state, we lack the capability to free them from that. Neither, indeed, do the most powerful of samsaric beings have any such ability, precisely because they themselves are still imprisoned within cyclic existence.

Even shravakas and solitary realisers, lacking great compassion and therefore attached to their own personal liberation, do not have this power. Only a buddha, possessing a wisdom that comprehends the nature of phenomena, a compassion that embraces all beings without partiality, and an energy that is inexhaustible, is able to do this. Since this is the case, one must respond to beings' sufferings by resolving to obtain buddhahood, the very fulfilment of one's buddha-nature. With such a resolution, bodhichitta is born and can subsequently be formalised in the bodhisattva vow.

Bodhichitta and the bodhisattva vow that expresses it possess two phases, one of aspiration and one of application. As it is said in *Entering the Bodhisattva Conduct*:

In brief, bodhichitta should be understood to be of two types: aspiration and application. As is understood by the distinction between aspiring to go and going, so the wise understand in turn the distinction between these two.[58]

Just as the previous blessed ones gave birth to bodhichitta, and just as they successively dwelt in the bodhisattva practices, likewise, for the sake of all beings, I give birth to bodhichitta and likewise shall too successively follow the practices.[59]

A valuable pair of meditations that may be utilised here are those known as 'equalising oneself with others' and 'exchanging oneself for others'. They are remedies for the habitual self-cherishing attitude which might otherwise undermine the bodhichitta of application.

As Sakya Pandita states:

There are three stages in cultivating bodhichitta— equalising of self and others, exchanging of self and others and the means of perfecting these two.[60]

Thus we begin with 'equalising'.

As it is said in *Entering the Bodhisattva Conduct*:

First of all I should strive to meditate upon the equality of myself and others. I should protect

all beings as I do myself, since we are all equal in
wanting pleasure and not wanting pain.[61]

So, considering that, just like oneself, all sentient beings
wish to be happy, one should help them to achieve such
happiness, together with its causes. Furthermore, thinking
that, just like oneself, all beings want to be free from
suffering, one should also help them achieve that state.
In time, all one's justifications for privileging oneself over
others will dissolve in these simple yet overpowering
reflections.

With such a surrender of one's claim to 'specialness',
one can afford to open one's heart to others completely in
the second bodhichitta meditation: 'exchanging oneself for
others'. This practice is known as 'the secret teaching of the
Mahayana'. As it says in *Entering the Bodhisattva Conduct*:

Those who quickly wish to afford protection to
themselves and others should practise the supreme
secret of exchanging oneself for others.[62]

As we have seen, it is our habitual self-clinging and its
emotional ally, self-cherishing, which blocks the flourishing
of compassion in one's life. However, if one actually
examines this 'self' to which one is so attached, one can see
that it is a mere conceptual imputation upon the sperm,
ovum and attaching consciousness that came together at
the moment of one's conception. There is no such intrinsic
identity there. It is merely that one has projected the
notion of self, that is to say—an autonomous, unchanging,
singular identity—upon this phenomenon which is, in
actuality, just the momentary uniting of various conditions.
That being so, such a label of 'self' might just as validly be
projected upon any such aggregation of sperm, ovum and
consciousness, such as those apparently belonging to other
beings. After all, in reality it is the temporary aggregation

of such elements that is the only basis for the projection of such a label as 'my self'.

Armed with this understanding of the notion of 'self' as merely a dependently arisen phenomenon, one can now utilise the very instability of self-identity in the technique of 'exchanging self for others'. In other words, one can transfer the notion of 'self' on to others, and thus take others as being oneself, object of all one's care and cherishing. In this way, one can reverse one's habitual perception and now see oneself as another and others as oneself.

With this strategic reorientation of one's perceptions, one will come to cherish others with the same intimacy and intensity which one had previously lavished upon oneself, since they have now become that very self. Emotions such as envy, competition and pride, which arise in the wake of self-cherishing, are also integrated into, and liberated in, this practice. They too are now directed towards the benefit of one's 'new self', that is to say, other beings, and thus counter to one's habitual cherishing of oneself.

> Considering lesser beings and so forth as myself, and considering myself as the other, I should meditate upon envy, competitiveness and pride with a mind freed from concepts.[63]

Through this exchange of self for others, the sufferings and causes of sufferings experienced by other beings become one's own and the force of one's virtuous actions and the resulting happiness are surrendered to them:

> May all the sufferings of the three realms ripen in myself. By the blessing of this virtue may all sentient beings attain buddhahood.[64]

A particularly effective way of meditating on this exchange is to link the taking of others' sufferings and the sending of one's happiness to them to the inhalation and exhalation of breath. When one breathes in, one should imagine that their sufferings and sins are inhaled into oneself in the form of smoke and, on the out breath, one should visualise all one's virtues and happiness in the form of moon-rays or sun-rays flowing to those beings. This technique of 'sending and taking' (Tib. *tong-len*) is at the heart of the mind-training instructions brought to Tibet by Atisha and now spread throughout all the traditions.

One's practice of equalising and exchanging will also be stabilised and extended, in between sessions of meditation practice, by applying the instructions on general moral conduct taught for holders of the bodhisattva vow. In particular, one should strive to accomplish the six perfections and the four means of gathering (giving, appropriate speech, guiding beings in accord with their situation and acting in accord with the dharma). As they have been taught in numerous sources, such as Sakya Pandita's *Elucidating the Thought of the Sage*, it is not necessary to detail them here.

Atisha

Five
The Crystal Key

Ultimate bodhichitta

Such compassionate conventional bodhichitta diminishes our self-clinging attitudes but it does not eradicate them totally. For this we require the clear vision of 'ultimate bodhichitta'. Now, if one were to ask at this point: 'What is this ultimate bodhichitta?', the actual reply is that it is simply the mind in its unfabricated nature. Nevertheless, it is presently unrecognised by sentient beings and elaborated by philosophers in a variety of mistaken ways, whether it be the 'self' and 'God' of the non-Buddhists or 'the five aggregates' and 'the truly established mind' of the Shravakas and Chittamatrins.

As Konchog Lhundrup declares:

All these are imputations which grasp at a conceptual extreme. In fact, the root of both samsara and nirvana is primordial mind, which, from the very beginning, has remained free of conceptual extremes. This is the ultimate bodhichitta.[65]

One approaches such ultimate bodhichitta through the step-by-step development of calm-abiding (Skt *shamatha*; Tib. *zhinay*) and insight (Skt. *vipashyana*; Tib. *lhagtong*). With the latter, one will be able to cut through all knots to reveal the unfabricated true nature of mind. However, without the presence of calm-abiding, our insight would be mere conceptual posturing. As it says in *Entering the Bodhisattva Conduct*:

> Having understood that disturbing emotions are completely overcome by insight endowed with calm-abiding, first of all I should seek calm-abiding.[66]

CALM ABIDING MEDITATION

The essence of calm-abiding meditation is one-pointed settling of mind, in which habitual dichotomising mental chatter and emotional tension come to rest in stillness. As it says in the *Jewel Cloud Sutra*:

> What is calm-abiding? It is one-pointedness of mind.[67]

When calm-abiding arises in one's meditation, one simply rests in the spaciousness of mind that has manifested with the stilling of the waves of conceptualisation and unruly emotions. However, for most people, such uncontrived calmness does not come about automatically. For this reason, it is useful to train in the various skilful means of stabilising the mind until obstacles fall away and this effortless calmness reveals itself.

However, even prior to practising the various stages of settling the mind, one should have some knowledge of the five major pitfalls to practice.

Laziness, forgetfulness of instructions
'Sinking' with dullness and 'scattering' with inattentiveness

Not applying remedial factors when necessary in
   one's meditation
And applying such remedies when they are no longer
   needed.

The specific antidotes to the first obstacle are the development of faith, effort, aspiration and flexibility; the remedies for forgetfulness are mindfulness and clear comprehension. This latter pair of antidotes also allows us to recognise and correct the twin obstacles of 'sinking and scattering'. Finally, the remedies to the fourth and fifth obstacles are found by the appropriate deployment of their counter factor—thus, non-application counters over-application and vice versa.

Equipped with knowledge of these common problems and their remedies, one can practise the nine stages of settling the mind:

Settling—Having adopted the correct meditation posture, one should focus on a suitable visual object of concentration such as a buddha image, a blue flower, a blue silken cloth, or a syllable such as the letter A. If a visual object is not conducive to settling, one could focus upon counting and following the breaths, a technique taught in many sources.

Continual Settling—Since beginners cannot concentrate for long periods, it is most suitable to practise in short but frequent sessions.

Resettling—When attention wanders, one redirects the mind to the object.

Perfect settling—Employing mindfulness, one should place the mind completely on the object.

Subduing—If 'sinking' through drowsiness arises at this stage, one should 'raise' the mind by lifting one's gaze and focussing upon the clear sky. If 'scattering' through inattention is the problem, one should instil a sense of 'groundedness' by lowering one's gaze or meditating in a darkened room.

Pacifying—If distraction creates a feeling of unease in one's meditation, or if a wish to discontinue arises, one should stabilise the mind by holding it strongly on the object.

Perfectly Pacifying—Likewise, when powerful opponents of meditation such as desire or malevolence develop, one pacifies the mind by employing remedies. In this respect, if one's meditation is obstructed by strong hatred, one should meditate on loving-kindness. If one is troubled by desires, one applies the remedy of contemplating the 'impure' or compounded nature of the object of longing. If one is afflicted by ignorance, one contemplates dependent origination and, if one is plagued by excessive conceptualisation, one should count and follow the breath.

One-pointedness—If hindrances remain to the full achievement of calmness, one should settle the mind directly on the thoughts themselves, thus integrating them into one's meditation.

Even settling—Through the practice of the preceding stages, the mind will eventually come to rest effortlessly in itself. When this happens, the skilful device of focussing upon an object is no longer necessary. One's meditation becomes relaxed and simple and one's mind is both flexible and clear. One is now ready to enter into insight meditation.

INSIGHT MEDITATION

Insight, through which the ultimately selfless nature of all phenomena is discerned, constitutes the actual practice of the perfection of wisdom. It is this wisdom which transforms all practice into the path. Without wisdom, the other five perfections of the Mahayana—giving, morality, patience, energy and meditation—will not lead one to buddhahood. Thus, as Chandrakirti says in *Entering the Middle Way*:

> Just as a group of blind men are easily led by a single man who can see the desired place, so here also, taking the qualities with the eye of intellect, one goes to the state of the victors.[68]

In the Shravakayana, insight only uproots the deluded notion of self as it is projected on to the individual person (Skt. *pudgala*; Tib. *gangzag*). However, here in the Mahayana, it also cuts through the delusion of selfhood or true existence in regard to any phenomenon (Skt. *dharma*; Tib. *cho*) whatsoever, thus laying bare their essential emptiness. Such realisation is often termed 'the mother of all buddhas', as one cannot become a buddha except through this wisdom, which brings to an end all our mistaken imputations concerning the world.

Regarding this two-fold nature of selflessness, it says in *Entering the Middle Way*:

> Selflessness is [taught] for the liberation of beings. Phenomena and the individual person are said to be the two types [of selflessness]. Therefore the Teacher taught the disciples according to these divisions.[69]

According to my masters, insight meditation leading to the realisation of this two-fold selflessness is to be practised in three stages:

Analysing the self in the individual
Analysing all appearances as mind
Analysing emptiness free from extremes.

Analysing the self in the individual

When commencing insight meditation, one should allow one's mind to settle—limpid yet clear, as it has become during calm-abiding meditation. In this state of stillness, one should analyse the idea of a personal self: an autonomous, discrete, unchanging and controlling identity which, at this moment, is the object of our strongest grasping.

If there were such a self to be found, it would necessarily be connected with either one's body, one's name or one's mind. However, to assert that the body is the location of the self is contradictory since the body, being a compound and impermanent phenomenon, cannot fulfil the functional requirements of singularity, permanence and autonomy. Likewise, to assert that one's name constitutes the self is an error, since name, being merely a linguistic convention, utterly lacks the characteristics of autonomy and permanence. Furthermore, since one's mind is continually changing, it cannot therefore be postulated as a locus of the self. Even if one were to insist that a new mental self was established at each successive moment, one would still be mistaken, since the very notion of a present moment involving, as it necessarily must, the three phases of beginning, middle and end, is infinitely divisible. One can therefore never reach a definitive 'present moment', and the notion of a 'self', predicated on the basis of such a moment, is untenable.

So, after this investigation of its possible locations, it is now possible to understand that the personal self which is imputed on the name, body or mind, exists only in the way in which a snake exists when a coloured rope is misperceived as a snake by a short-sighted man.

At this point in one's meditation, one might imagine, as the Shravakas belonging to the Vaibhashika and the Sautrantika tenet-systems do, that, although there is no personal self to be found, nevertheless there are truly existent phenomena comprising momentary, yet inherently existent, irreducible physical particles and irreducible moments of mind and associated mental functions— all arising in patterns of interaction and immediately disintegrating like the forms in a kaleidoscope. Although such a view is superior to those of non-Buddhists, with their grasping at the true existence of a personal self, it is nonetheless mistaken from the point of view of ultimate truth, as it still attributes true existence to phenomena, and thus leaves a basis for grasping. As it says in *Entering the Bodhisattva Conduct*:

> Furthermore, among the yogins, there are differences in understanding. Those with higher views contradict those with lower views.[70]

Analysing all appearances as mind

Continuing in meditation therefore, one should now thoroughly examine all phenomena, even the most seemingly minute or subtle, whether apparently physical or apparently mental, until one recognises that the basis of all appearances is simply mind. As Lord Buddha declared in *The Ten Levels Sutra:*

> The three realms are just mind, sons of the Conqueror.[71]

Those phenomena, which one assumes to have an independent external existence have, in reality, been established by mind—rather like dream appearances which, although fascinating or fearsome at the time, are recognised as simply projections of the mind, when one awakens. One should ask oneself: 'How can any difference be found between dream experience and everyday life experience?' Both sets of appearances are simply arising due to the ripening of karmic imprints carried in the mind and now stimulated to arise, whether as 'dream' or 'everyday life', by the gathering of the appropriate conditions. In reality, there is nothing truly existent external to and separate from the mind, not least because such a separate object would not be apprehendable by the mind, since it would, perforce, lack any connection with it whatsoever.

Even the irreducible physical particles posited by Vaibhashikas and Sautrantikas as the basis of apparent objects are found, when analysed, to be devoid of inherent existence and to have been established in dependence on mind. If one considers this point, one will realise that such an 'irreducible' entity, in order to be able to constitute, in agglomeration with other such entities, the basis of perceptible objects, would have to possess internal and external dimensions and therefore be compounded of parts. Since this is so, the notion of a partless and therefore irreducible entity is impossible. Such an entity can only exist as a projection of mind.

One should also scrutinise the appearance of a variety of objects, such as water, food, faces and bodies. In each case one will conclude, as before, that each phenomenon has been established through the power of imprints or tendencies that condition the mind to manifest as a particular appearance. In the case of water, for instance, one will understand that what appears as water to most humans would occur to the gods of the desire-realms as nectar, but to the beings in hell it would arise as molten iron and weapons.

As Asanga declares:

Since a single object is seen differently
In accordance with the class of being to which one
  belongs,
Such as hungry ghost, animal, human or god,
It cannot be accepted as truly existent.[72]

At this point, to accept that the object, external appearances, are ultimately non-existent, because they are none other than mind, but that mind, the perceiving subject, is ultimately existent, is to continue to err. In fact, if the object, the external world, cannot be established as inherently existent, equally and obviously, the subject, the perceiving consciousness, cannot be established as such either. Without an object, how can there be a subject? Both subject and object are mutually dependent projections of mind itself.

As Vasubandhu says:

Because the object does not exist, there is no subject.[73]
However, although such an understanding that the mind is empty of the duality of subject and object as maintained in the Chittamatra tenet-system is indeed profound, it does not constitute complete insight and still leaves a basis for grasping, in that the mind is still considered a truly existent entity. One should thus persevere in meditation until the view is perfected in the Madhyamaka.

Analysing the emptiness free from extremes

Look at mind itself in meditation. Like a crystal, it reflects all the appearances of the phenomenal world, yet one cannot find any identifiable essence to it. Examine it for its colour: is it yellow, blue, red, or green? Its shape: is it oblong, square, circular or triangular? Its location: is it inside or outside the body, or somewhere in between? From whence does it originate? Where does it endure right now and where will it go? In each case one will realise that, upon analysis, no identifiable essence can be found. It is empty of colour, shape or location. It has no point of origination, destination, and no duration in the present moment. The more one searches for essence, the more elusive this becomes, until one concludes that it is entirely unfindable.

Yet if one were now to conclude that mind, like the child of a barren woman, is simply non-existent, one would be falling into the deluded extremist view of annihilationism by mistaking mind's essential emptiness for a mere nothingness. For mind, although it cannot be discovered anywhere, is the very ground for the manifestation of the phenomenal world. Thus, while it cannot be termed 'existent' since it is devoid of the attributes of existence, it cannot be non-existent either, since if it were non-existent there would be no appearances whatsoever. It follows that it cannot be simultaneously both existent and non-existent, since both of these assertions have been disproved individually. Fourthly and finally, any other assertion about mind cannot be sustained either, because it would necessarily be a position dependent for its formulation upon an existence and non-existence that have already been refuted.

Exaggerations and denigrations of mind's nature in eternalist or annihilationist terms such as 'truly existent' or 'truly non-existent' entirely fall away with this recognition of its unelaborated nature, just as fears that may be imagined in darkness vanish when seen in the light of day. Indeed, now one realises that trying to locate or objectify the mind in any way whatsoever is utterly mistaken, like attempting to affix labels to space. With this understanding, one can simply relax at ease—whatever appearances or thoughts arise need not be grasped or rejected, since they are no more than the play of this space-like mind, ultimate bodhichitta. Such is the authentic insight meditation.

Now one brings together the selfless compassion arising from meditation on conventional bodhichitta and the selfless wisdom springing from meditation on ultimate bodhichitta, realising that this union of compassion and emptiness is the very essence of bodhichitta and the very core of the Mahayana path. As such, through compassion, it doesn't fall into the trap of the shravakas' attachment to the mere cessation of personal suffering, and, through wisdom, it does not remain in samsara, since the objects of compassion are not perceived as substantially existent entities.

Up to this point, the instructions presented here on the four thoughts and the two bodhichittas parallel those given as the entire course of instructions in *Parting from the Four Attachments*, those given up to and including the generation of 'the common experiential vision' in *The Path and its Result*, those given to 'the superior person' according to Atisha's *Lamp of the Path of Enlightenment* and those taught in Gampopa's *Jewel Ornament of Liberation*.

Drakpa Gyaltsen

Six
The Path of the Emperor

Practising Vajrayana

Once some experience of the two bodhichittas has developed, one should enter into this third vehicle, the Vajrayana, because it is only the system of the Uncommon Mahayana that makes it possible to achieve buddhahood in one life, whereas, by employing the methods of the Common Mahayana alone, such a result would only be gained after many lifetimes. However, to practise the Vajrayana methods effectively, one needs to follow the pattern taught in the tantras themselves, thus receiving the requisite initiations from qualified masters, maintaining the vows transmitted in those initiations and gaining accomplishment by subsequently practising meditation.

The Vajrayana is often termed 'the system that takes the result as the path'. The implication of such a designation can be explained as follows: it is taught in the tantras that, since the natural purity of mind has never been compromised in any way by its adventitious obscurations, the wisdom of enlightenment already exists in all sentient beings (a point that we touched upon briefly in Chapter

Two). Consequently, the result, buddhahood, is not to be found external to our mind. In fact, mind is actually the causal basis of samsara and nirvana—when unrecognised, it is the ground upon which appear all the manifestations of samsara, but, when recognised, it is the ground upon which appear all the qualities of nirvana. Thus the method of the Vajrayana path itself is to recognise and settle in that basis. The result, buddhahood, will then arise as simply the manifestation of the enlightened potency of mind.

As Zhalu Losal Tenchong declares:

Since the mind itself is the basis of samsara and nirvana, and since, from the conceptual mind of a sentient being up to the bodies, wisdoms and activities of a buddha's mind, all appear as an unbroken continuum, it is known as 'tantra' (i.e. 'continuum').[74]

And:

When one looks into the essence of mind—clear, aware and empty—it is unchanging, but, when one looks into its differentiations, it is changing.[75]

The following analogy might help to clarify this point: a piece of copper can be fashioned in distinct ways and thus serve as a chamber-pot, an incense holder or a statue of the Buddha, but the essence of the copper itself does not change in the slightest. Similarly, whether a hell-being or a buddha, the essence of mind does not change. However, from the perspective of conventional truth, there is the appearance to sentient beings of the suffering, actions, causes and effects that are known as 'the six realms of samsara', the various experiences that arise on the path for yogins and, finally, the arrival at buddhahood.

At this point, some might wonder whether this Vajrayana presentation of the view differs from the description of mind in the Common Mahayana. However, when this question is examined, it becomes clear that there is no real contradiction between the two in terms of the actual nature of mind that is the object of the view but that there is a difference in the methods employed to realise the mind's nature.

As Sakya Pandita declared:

While a gradation of views does exist between the two systems of Shravaka and Mahayana, no such distinction is taught between the systems of the Perfections and Mantra. If there existed any view higher than the non-elaboration of the Perfections system, such a view would be elaborated, and if, on the other hand, they are both non-elaborated, there can be no difference between them. Thus the view to be understood is the same in both systems. Nevertheless, the Mantra system has superior means for realising the unelaborated.[76]

Therefore, since the Common Mahayana system depends mostly upon conceptual analysis, it is very difficult to produce more than a proximate understanding of the unelaborated nature of mind. However, in Vajrayana, the method of realising the view does not rely upon such conceptualisation but upon the special means constituted by the blessings received in initiations.

As Sonam Tsemo says:

In the Secret Mantra path, at the moment of the descent of transcendental wisdom or at the time of the third initiation (in anuttara tantra), transcendental wisdom is born in one's mind. Thus Vajrayana practitioners genuinely realise the unelaborated. Therefore this system is superior.[77]

The four sets of tantras

Such is the view to be realised through the methods of
Vajrayana. Now it is appropriate to discuss the tantras,
source of the Vajrayana view and methods, and how they
are to be ordered. As was mentioned earlier, the tantras
were originally revealed in pure realms and then later
spread in our world by Shakyamuni Buddha and various
sambhogakaya forms of the Buddha. Their principal
contents are the mandalas and ritual methods for
accomplishing various deities, each of which is expressive
of the fundamental qualities of enlightened mind itself. It
is precisely because of this last point that deity-yoga, which
will be discussed below, is the supreme means for gaining
accomplishment.

Although it is taught that countless tantras have been
proclaimed, not all were transmitted in our world, and,
of those that were, not all have survived. Later scholars in
India and Tibet have arranged those which are still extant in
a number of sets reflecting their particular characteristics.
In Tibet itself, although followers of the 'ancient tantra'
school ordered their tantric scriptures in six sets, most
great scholars of the 'new tantra schools'—Sakya, Kagyu
and Gelug—prefer to group them in four sets: kriya, charya,
yoga and anuttarayoga.

As Sonam Tsemo says:

The four sets of tantras are for the different levels
of practitioners. The person of inferior ability
enjoys external practices of purity and so on. For
such practitioners, the Teacher taught the external
practices of the kriya tantras. The charya tantras
were taught for people who are superior to such
practitioners and therefore like both external
practices related to body and speech as well as
inner meditation. The yoga tantras were taught for

superior people who mainly like inner meditation, and, for the supreme practitioners who like the highest meditation, anuttara tantras were taught. Due to the fact that this tradition of explanation is taken from the Vajrapanjara tantra and was maintained by the great siddhas Virupa and Dombi Heruka, it is the best explanation.[78]

Accordingly, in the kriya ('activity') tantras there are ritual activities and requirements concerning purity and diet. In the meditations of this tantra set, one does not visualise oneself as the deity but venerates an external image of the deity, together with reciting the requisite mantra to invoke his or her blessing. Kriya tantra deities are classed in three primary groups. Thus in the tathagata family the chief deity to be meditated upon is Manjushri, embodiment of the wisdom of all buddhas; in the vajra family it is Vajrapani, embodiment of the power of all buddhas, and in the padma family it is Avalokiteshvara, embodiment of the compassion of all buddhas. In fact, the most important major initiation of this system is that given for these three deities in a single mandala where they are known as 'The Lords of the Three Families'.

The charya ('conduct') tantras are for those who wish to practise both external and internal activities, thus combining some of the kriya tantra's emphasis on purity with the yoga tantra's focus upon meditation. In the meditations of this tantra set, one visualises oneself in the pledge-form (Skt. *samayasattva*; Tib. *damtsigpa*) of the deity and visualises the wisdom-being (Skt. *jnanasattva*; Tib. *yeshepa*) of the deity in front. Among the most important initiations in the charya set is that for Manjushri Arapatsana in a mandala of five deities.

The yoga tantras emphasise internal meditation over external activity. In such meditation, having visualised oneself as the pledge-deity, one 'invites' the wisdom-being of the deity to pervade oneself for the duration of the meditation session. Among the various major initiations and cycles of practice in this tantra set is that for Vairochana Sarvavid.

However, although such differences exist between the perspectives and methods of these three tantra sets, when one practices their deity-yogas as they appear in such celebrated collections as that of Bari Lotsava (1040–1123), the actual sadhanas ('methods of accomplishment') to be employed are patterned on the template found in the yoga tantras.

As Sakya Pandita explains:

Extant sadhanas that do include self-creation (as the deity) have been modelled on the practices of the yoga tantra.[79]

In fact, the practice of deity-yoga in these three lower tantra sets is aimed only indirectly at buddhahood, being aimed primarily at the acquisition of the 'magical' or mundane accomplishments (Skt. *laukika siddhi*). The latter are usually delineated as 'the four actions', that gather the necessary conditions for practising the path with ease and swiftness.

As Atisha says:

Through the actions of pacifying and increasing and the rest brought about by the power of mantra, it is maintained that the accumulations of enlightenment are perfected with ease.[80]

The four are: (1) pacifying disturbances, (2) increasing the conditions of intelligence, longevity, prosperity and mastery, (3) magnetising beings and auspicious circumstances and, finally, (4) forcefully subjugating obstacles.

However, by contrast with the lower tantras, in the practice of the anuttarayoga tantra, with its skilful methods of the development and completion stages, one aims directly at buddhahood. Indeed, it is only through the union of these two meditative processes that there is the dawning of the The Great Seal wisdom, which wisdom itself is the transcendental accomplishment (Skt. *lokuttara siddhi*) and the supreme realisation of the Vajrayana path.

As Sonam Tsemo says:

> The anuttarayoga tantra set is so named because there a special incomparable (Skt. *anuttara*) meditation is taught.[81]

Anuttarayoga is itself divided into three sub-sets: 'father-line' tantras, 'mother-line' tantras and 'non-dual' tantras, each having its particular tantras and its own particular orientation in spiritual practice. In this regard: 'Father' tantras, such as Guhyasamaja and Vajrabhairava, emphasise skilful means; 'mother' tantras such as Chakrasamvara and Mahamaya emphasise wisdom; and non-dual tantras, such as Hevajra and Kalachakra, are those in which both [skilful] means and wisdom are jointly emphasised.

The method of practice

In order to practice the deity-yogas contained in any of the four tantra sets it is necessary to receive the relevant initiation.

As Sakya Pandita states:

> If one has set out in Vajrayana and quickly wishes to achieve buddhahood, one should exert oneself in 'ripening' and 'liberating'. The factor that ripens is initiation and so one should seek out and take

the four initiations from a master whose lineage of instructions is unbroken.[82]

And:

If one wishes to cultivate the mantra path one must unerringly obtain the four initiations, meditate upon the two stages and become well-versed in The Great Seal, the transcendental wisdom that arises from them.[83]

As to the nature of an initiation, Sakya Pandita defines it as follows:

Initiation is a name given to a technique for becoming enlightened in this very life after the seeds of buddhahood have been planted within one's aggregates, elements and sense-bases. Therefore it is taught that a person of superior faculties may be liberated through initiation alone. Others whom initiation cannot liberate need cultivation through meditation. Thus 'meditation' is a name for the safeguarding and increase of what was obtained in initiation. Therefore, just as, in the Perfections Vehicle, there is no other dharma than bodhichitta, for one who enters Vajrayana there is no dharma but initiation.[84]

Despite the term 'initiation' (and sometimes 'empowerment') being employed in a loose sense nowadays, one should distinguish between 'permission initiations' (Tib. jenang) and the 'major initiations' (Tib. wongkur; Skt. abhisheka). Both are found in all four classes of tantras. In a 'permission initiation', the lama blesses the body, speech and mind of those present at the initiation, so the disciples can cultivate identification with these three aspects of the buddha-deity of the initiation. However, there is no formal entry into a mandala. By contrast, major initiations in all four tantra sets are bestowed within a mandala. Thus, in the kriya tantra, one is led into a mandala, the palace of the buddha-deity, where the 'water' and 'crown' initiations are bestowed. In major initiations of the charya set, the initiations of 'water', 'crown', 'vajra', 'bell' and 'name' are given. In the yoga tantras, the vajra-master initiation is given in addition to the five found in the charya tantras. Finally, in anuttarayoga tantra, in addition to these initiations from the yoga tantra set, three higher initiations, those of 'secret', 'wisdom' and the 'fourth', are bestowed. Furthermore, in the Sakya tradition, a 'blessing initiation' (Tib. *jinlab*) authorising the disciples to meditate on the goddess Vajrayogini may be bestowed once the disciples have received a major initiation of an anuttara tantra 'mother-line' tantra.

Once one has received initiation, textual transmission and instructions[85] from a lama who holds these in an unbroken line from his own masters, one must then maintain the vows (Skt. *samvara* Tib. *dom*) and sacred pledges (Skt. *samaya* Tib. *dam-tsig*) received at the time of the initiation itself. In the two lower tantra sets the vows are those taken over from the Shravakayana and Mahayana, namely the vow of individual liberation and the bodhisattva vow. However, if one receives a major initiation in a mandala of the yoga and anuttarayoga tantras, in addition to these common vows, one observes the specific vow of Vajrayana, which is embodied in the commitment to avoid the fourteen root downfalls[86] and so preserve the pure vision to which one is introduced at the time of initiation.

In each of the tantra sets one practises deity (Tib. *yidam*) yoga by the three methods of mantra, mudra ('gesture') and meditation. Through these three methods, one's impure vision of ordinary body, speech and mind is transformed into the pure vision in which they are seen as the 'the three gates' of the deity. Although the deity and its mandala are to be experienced in vivid clarity, at the same time, they are not something ontologically existent. As that is so, cultivating 'pride' in our identity as the deity functions as the antidote to the ordinary conceptualisation of self and the disturbing emotion of pride, which are the workings of impure vision.

Furthermore, by reliance on such deity-yoga, the Vajrayana meditator need not reject whatever objects arise, whereas for the ordinary practitioner sense-objects are poisons, inimical to liberation, since they prompt attachment. In Vajrayana, through the practice of arising as the deity in the development-stage or gaining control of the mind and inner elements through the completion-stage, one can experience objects as pure appearance, apparent but simultaneously empty. In such a way, the compulsion to grasp them ceases and they are transformed into factors that strengthen one's meditative concentration.

As it says in the *Guhyasamaja tantra:*

> You should rely on the enjoyment of all sense-objects as you wish by means of the practice of your deity.[87]

And as Sonam Tsemo says:

> If one questions whether one will not be bound by objects, the answer is that ordinary beings who do not possess skilful means will be bound by them but, for those who do possess skilful means, they will become aids to liberation.[88]

And:

> Here by those with skilful means the wavering of the mind is brought to cessation. Since Guhyamantra has many skilful and easy practices, it is superior.[89]

The specific iterations of the method of practising Vajrayana vary across the extant traditions. Thus, in the new tantra tradition as maintained by the Sakya, Ngor and Tsar lineages, the chief practices of the anuttara tantra are the six-limbed meditation of Shri Hevajra associated with the *The Path and its Result* and the development and completion-stage meditations of Narotapa's Vajrayogini, together with their accompanying preliminary practices comprising refuge and bodhichitta, Vajrasattva recitation, mandala-offering and guru-yoga. In addition to these two major cycles, the Sakya school is also famed for such esoteric teachings as *The Thirteen Golden Dharmas*, which contain not only three cycles of Vajrayogini but also the meditations of such deities as Shri Dzambhala and the godddess Kurukulla, whose practices bestow 'mundane' accomplishments like 'increasing' and 'attracting'.[90]

Whilst all branches of the second new tantra tradition, the Dakpo Kagyu, practise related systems of mahamudra and the 'six doctrines of Naro', the Karma-Kagyu school practises them alongside guru-yogas focussed upon the figures of Marpa, Mila, Gampopa and Karmapa and the deity-yoga practices of Vajravarahi, Chakrasamvara and Jinasagara. A number of Kagyu meditators also utilise the practice of Severance (Tib. *chod*), a cycle blending The Perfection of Wisdom with Vajrayana, which derives from the lineage of the Indian yogin Phadampa Sanjay and the Tibetan yogini Machik Labdron (1055–1149).

The Geluk, the third and final of the surviving 'new tantra' schools, focusses chiefly on Vajrabhairava, Guhyasamaja and Chakrasamvara, the principal meditation-deities of its founder, Tsongkhapa, who was indebted to a wide range of masters from the other schools—Sakya, Kagyu and Kadam—in addition to a number of minor lines such as that of the celebrated scholar, Buton Rinchen Drup (1290–1364).

By contrast with 'new tantra' traditions, the Nyingma school has a somewhat distinctive spiritual syllabus, as is evidenced in the cycles of instructions revealed by such masters as Rikdzin Jigme Lingpa, Rikdzin Jatson Nyingpo and Chogyur Dechen Lingpa (1829–1870). Its key Vajrayana practices are those of the 'three inner tantras'—maha, anu and ati—prefaced by the accomplishment of the five-fold preliminary meditations similar to those employed in the Sakya and Kagyu traditions. Maha-yoga consists of meditation upon either Padmakara in the form of lama, deity and dakini, or upon a deity from the 'eight words of practice' cycle such as Vajrakilaya. The chief focus of anu-yoga is completion-stage meditation upon the subtle inner body of channels, winds and drops. Finally, in ati-yoga, the practitioner recognise and settles in the primordial purity of empty awareness through 'direct cutting' (Tib. *tregcho*) and then perfects the inherent luminosity of awareness as the bodies and wisdoms of a buddha in 'leap over' (Tib. *thogal*).

The result of Vajrayana practice

In the Common Mahayana, in contrast to the Vajrayana, not only is it difficult to realise the profound view, but it is also necessary to exert great discipline in controlling one's senses. In addition, relatively few means are taught by which one might gather the accumulations of merit and wisdom. As a result, the shortest time in which the attainment of buddhahood can be gained on this path is three incalculable aeons. However, in Vajrayana, by contrast, this result can either be reached in this lifetime, in the intermediate-state following death, in seven lifetimes or, at most, in sixteen lifetimes.

As Sonam Tsemo says:

> One might ask when the result is obtained in Vajrayana. An excellent person will achieve it in this very life, a mediocre one in the intermediate state, an inferior one in seven lifetimes and an extremely inferior one after sixteen lifetimes.[91]

And:

> Because the result is achieved without difficulties, it is termed "The Resultant Vehicle."[92]

Through the practice of these extraordinarily skilful teachings of the tantras, one can gather the two accumulations of merit and primordial wisdom with ease. Equipped with these provisions for the spiritual journey, one will swiftly traverse the inner five paths and thirteen levels until, on the thirteenth level itself, one will attain the stage of Vajradhara Buddha. Here, the ocean of birth and death will have evaporated, since its cause, unawareness of the true nature of mind, will have disappeared. Mind's nature—emptiness and clarity—stripped of its obscurations will now shine resplendent as the kayas and wisdoms performing unceasing compassionate activity for the benefit of all.

Until such attainment, one should make the following aspiration:

> Throughout all lifetimes may I never be separate
>   from the perfect lama
> And thus enjoy the glorious dharma.
> Perfecting the qualities of the paths and levels,
> May I attain the state of Vajradhara.

Completed originally by Lama Jampa Thaye on 3 January 1989, the anniversary of the Lord of Dharma, Jamgon Kongtrul, with prayers that the glorious teachings of Buddha might spread throughout the world, bringing joy and liberation to all beings. This new edition was completed in Los Angeles on the anniversary of Manjushri Sakya Pandita, January 2022.

Notes

1   As detailed by Sonam Tsemo in *The General System of Tantra Sets*.

2   Maitreya / Asanga, *The Supreme Continuum Treatise*, p.23a.

3   In later Buddhist history, a number of different presentations of Madhyamaka have been transmitted, chief amongst them being the Svatantrika and Prasangika which arose in India between the fifth and seventh centuries C.E. In Tibet one can discern three major lines of Madhyamaka thought, all of which stemmed from Indian antecedents but received their most pronounced form in Tibet. The first line, which may be termed 'The Madhyamaka free from extremes', includes such philosphers as Sakya Pandita, Gorampa and Rongtonpa (1367-1449) who utilised the approaches of both the Prasangika and Svatantrika schools in order to provide a coherent account of the two truths and avoid the extremes of both a subtle eternalism and a subtle annihilationism; the second line comprises the version of Prasangika expounded by Tsongkhapa and other Gelugpa scholars, wherein emptiness is defined as merely the lack of any intrinsic nature in any phenomena whatsoever; and the

third line is that of 'The Great Madhyamaka' or 'Zhentong Madhyamaka' maintained by thinkers such as the third and seventh Karmapas, Jamgon Kongtrul Lodro Thaye (1811–1899), Shakya Chogden and Dolpopa Sherab Gyaltsen. In this system, while all conditioned phenomena are seen as intrinsically empty (Tib. *rang tong*), the buddha-nature, the luminous nature of mind, is regarded as being the ultimately real; its emptiness merely consists in it being empty of everything other (Tib. *zhen tong*) than its own nature. Furthermore, whilst all other Madhyamikas hold the teachings of the 'second turning of the wheel' to be of definitive meaning (Skt. *nitartha*; Tib. *ngedon*), and those of the third turning to be only provisional (Skt. *neyartha*; Tib. *drangdon*), the zhentongpas, though viewing the 'second turning' as comprising a mixture of provisional and definitive teaching, see the 'third turning' in which buddha-nature was expounded as totally definitive and therefore expressive of Buddha's highest teachings.

4   Sonam Tsemo, op.cit., p.3.

5   In the new tantra schools the term The Great Seal (Skt. *mahamudra*) denotes the realisation of primordial wisdom attained through the unification of the 'development' and 'completion' stages of anuttara tantra practice.

6   On Yeshe Tsogyal see K. Dowman, *Sky Dancer*, Routledge, Boston, 1984.

7   According to this perspective, since all phenomena of samsara and nirvana are fundamentally empty, they are perfect as they are. Liberation therefore occurs through recognition of this utter purity which is coextensive with dharmakaya, the actual nature of awareness (Tib. *rigpa*).

8   The 'Six Doctrines of Naro' comprise the completion-stage yogas of heat, illusory body, luminosity, dream, transference and intermediate state, which are derived from various tantras such as Hevajra, Mahamaya, Chakrasamvara and Caturpitha.

9   Sakya Pandita, *Elucidating the Thought of the Sage*, p.7.

10 id., p.9.

11 As contained in the guru-yoga section of the lam-dre preliminaries entitled *The Excellent Path of the Two Accumulations*, p.43.

12 Nagarjuna, *Letter to a Friend*, p.64.

13 Sakya Pandita, *Discriminating the Three Vows*, p.54.

14 id., p.49.

15 As quoted in Tsarchen Losal Gyamtso, *The Fifty Verses on the Lama*, p.456-8.

16 id., p.428.

17 Maitreya / Asanga, *The Supreme Continuum Treatise*, p.4a.

18 Sonam Tsemo, op.cit., p.60.

19 On the 'five certainties' see Mipham Rinpoche, *The Gateway to Knowledge*, p.239.

20 The Abhidharma is the scriptural collection containing the systematic analysis of phenomena and the cataloguing of these into various groupings such as the aggregates, the twelve sense-bases and the eighteen elements.

21 The Vinaya is the scriptural collection of Buddha's teachings on moral discipline and the methods of bestowing the various Individual Liberation (Skt. pratimoksha) vows.

22 Sonam Tsemo, op.cit., p.159.

23 Having attained the path of vision, the third of the five paths that trace the journey to enlightenment in all three vehicles, one cannot fall back in one's progress to the goal.

24 An arhat (male) / arhati (female) is one who, by removing the obscuration formed of the disturbing emotions, has gained the highest spiritual realisation available in the lesser vehicle, the culmination of the four stages of perfection: stream-entrant, once-returner, non-returner and arhat.

25 A bodhisattva is one who, in generating bodhichitta, has dedicated himself or herself to the achievement of buddhahood for the benefit of sentient beings.

26 In the Mahayana, the 'levels' (Skt. *bhumi*; Tib. *sa*) denote the ten successive 'noble' levels attained by bodhisattvas who have achieved the decisive insight into reality that occurs on the 'path of vision'. Buddha detailed the qualities and practices relevant to each level in the *Dashabhumikasutra*, and Sakya Pandita has written extensively on the levels and the related topic of the five paths in his *Elucidating the Thought of the Sage*. The thirteen levels of the Vajrayana system are detailed in the *Path and its Result* literature.

27 On those vows see Chapter Six of *Rain of Clarity*.

28 See for instance Jamgon Kongtrul, *Torch of Certainty* and Patrul Rinpoche, *The Words of My Perfect Master*.

29 Ngorchen Konchog Lhundrup, op.cit., p.220.

30 There are two types of non-virtue: 'intrinsic non-virtues'—actions which when committed create suffering and are therefore inherently sinful—and those deeds which, otherwise neutral, become non-virtuous when committed by someone who holds a vow to abstain from them and which are thus characterised as 'acquired non-virtues'.

31 This text belongs to the cycle of *Parting from the Four Attachments*.

32 Ngorchen Konchog Lhundrup, op.cit., p.273.

33 id., p.274.

34 Shantideva, *Entering the Bodhisattva Conduct*, p.15b.

35 The five heinous actions, which, unless purified lead directly to the lower realms at death, are to slay one's father or mother, to slay an arhat, to maliciously draw blood from a buddha and to cause a schism in the monastic sangha.

36 Nagarjuna, op.cit., p.63.

37 Mipham Rinpoche, op.cit., p.11.

38 Shantideva, op.cit., pp.15a–15b.

39 Thogme Zangpo, *Thirty Seven Practices of a Buddha's Child*.

40 As quoted in Ngorchen Konchog Lhundrup, op.cit., p.288.

41 Nagarjuna, op.cit., p.60.

42 As quoted in Ngorchen Konchog Lhundrup, op.cit. p.301.

43 As quoted in Gampopa, *Jewel Ornament of Liberation*, p.43b.

44 id., p. 48b.

45 Patrul Rinpoche, op.cit., p.129.

46 Numerous texts, commencing with the various rescensions of the Vinaya, include abortion in their iteration of the non-virtuous act of taking human life.

47 Patrul Rinpoche, op.cit., p.113.

48 Jetsun Drakpa Gyaltsen, *Parting from the Four Attachments*, p.312.

49 As quoted in Ngorchen Konchog Lhundrup, *op.cit.*, p.58

50 id., p.258.

51 Sakya Pandita, *Elucidating the Thought of the Sage*, p.122.

52 Jetsun Drakpa Gyaltsen, op. cit., p.313.

53 Sakya Pandita, *Discriminating the Three Vows*, p.43.

54 Shantideva, op.cit., p.3a.

55 Sakya Pandita, *Elucidating the Thought of the Sage*, p.12.

56 Chogyal Phakpa, *The Garland of Jewels*, p.325.

57 Nagarjuna, op.cit., p.67.

58 Shantideva, op.cit., p.3b.

59 id., p. 13a.

60 Sakya Pandita, op. cit., p.82.

61 Shantideva, id., p.51b.

62 id., p.54a.

63 id., p.55b.

64 Jetsun Drakpa Gyaltsen, op.cit. p.313.

65 Ngorchen Konchog Lhundrup, op.cit. p.373.

66 Shantideva, op.cit., p.45a.

67 As quoted in Ngorchen Konchog Lhundrup, op.cit., p.180.

68 Chandrakirti, *Entering the Middle Way*, pp.12–13.

69 id., p.48.

70 Shantideva, op.cit., p.59b.

71 As cited in Ngorchen Konchog Lhundrup, op.cit., p.391.

72 id., p.392.

73 id., p.395.

74 Zhalu Losal Tenchong, *Showing the Dharmata*, p.424.

75 ibid.

76 Sakya Pandita, *Discriminating the Three Vows*, p.58.

77 Sonam Tsemo, op.cit., p.92.

78 id., p. 127

79 Sakya Pandita, *Discriminating the Three Vows*, p. 61.

80 Atisha, op. cit., p. 6.

81 Sonam Tsemo, op.cit., p.128.

82 Sakya Pandita, op.cit., p.35.

83 ibid.

84 id., p.43.

85 To be able to carry out the actual meditation practice of the deity received in an initiation it is also necessary to receive the reading transmission (Tib. *lung*) of the actual practice from one's lama. This takes the form of the lama reciting the words of the text to the student, conveying the blessing of the lineage through which the teaching has been transmitted. Although in Vajrayana one must receive the reading transmission for any text one might wish to study or practise, in the sutra teachings this is not considered to be quite as necessary. However, the reading transmission for many sutra texts still exists and it is certainly beneficial to receive such transmissions from one's lama since it nurtures one's realisation.

The third category of Vajrayana teaching following initiation and reading transmission is instruction (Tib. *tri*) in the actual techniques contained in the meditation practice. In many, though by no means all, cases, such instructions exist now in the form of commentaries based on the discourses of great masters of the lineage.

86 See *Rain of Clarity,* p.95.

87 Sonam Tsemo, op.cit., p.85.

88 id., p.84.

89 id., p.107.

90 The *'Thirteen Golden Dharmas'* comprise Naro Dakini, Maitri Dakini and Indra Dakini ('The Three Great Dakinis'), Kurukulla, Kamaraja and Ganapati ('The Three Great Reds'), Vasudhara, Tinuma and Garbhasuvarnasutrashri ('The Three Minor Reds'), Black Manjushri, Simhamukha, Vajra Garuda and Shri Dzambhala. In addition, White Amitayus, Simhanada and Ayurvajradevi are sometimes included.

91 Sonam Tsemo, op.cit., p.89.

92 id., p.90.

List of Tibetan Terms

Simplified spelling	Wylie transliteration
Baram	'Ba' rom
Baram Dorje Wangchuk	'Ba' rom rDo rje dBang phyug
chagya chenpo	phyag rgya chen po
Chapa Chokyi Sengge	Phya pa Chos kyi Seng ge
Chenrezik	sPyan ras gzigs
Cho	gCod
Chogyal Phakpa	Chos rgyal 'Phags pa
Chogyay Trichen	bCo brgyad Khri can
cho-ngon	chos mngon
Choyul	gCod yul
Dakpo Kagyu	Dwags po bKa' brgyud
Dakpo Lhaje	Dwags po Lha rje
Dalai Lama	Ta la'i bLa ma
damnag	gdams ngag
Dolma	sGrol ma
Dolpopa Sherab Gyaltsen	Dol po pa Shes rab rGyal mtshan
drachompa	dgra bcom pa

drangdon	drang don
Drepung	'Bras spungs
Drigung	'Bri gung
Drokmi Lotsava	'brog mi Lo tsa ba
Dromton	'Brom ston
Drukpa	'Brug pa
dulwa	'dul ba
Dusum Khyenpa	Dus gsum mKhyen pa
Dza Patrul	rDza dPal sprul
dzogchen / dzogpa chenpo	rdzogs chen / rdzogs pa chen po
Dzogchen Shenga	rDzogs chen gZhan dga'
Gampopa	sGam po pa
Ganden	dGa' ldan
Gandenpa	dGa' ldan pa
Gelug	dGe lugs
Gelugpa	dGe lugs pa
Gorampa Sonam Sengge	Go rams pa bSod nams Seng ge
Guru Rinpoche	Guru Rin po che
Gyalse Thogme	rGyal sras Thogs med
Gyaltsab	rGyal tshab
Gyalwa Karmapa	rGyal ba Karma pa
Jamgon Kongtrul Lodro Thaye	'Jam mgon Kong sprul bLo gros mTha' yas
Jamyang Khyentse Chokyi Lodro	'Jam dbyangs mKhyen brtse Chos kyi bLo gros
Jamyang Khyentse Wangpo	'Jam dbyangs mKhyen brtse'i dBang po
jangchup sempa	byang chub sems dpa'
jenang	rjes gnang
Jetsun Drakpa Gyaltsen	rJe btsun Grags pa rGyal mtshan
jinlab	byin rlabs
Kadam	bKa' gdams
Kadampa	bKa' gdams pa
Kagyu	bKa' brgyud
Karma Kagyu	Karma bKa' brgyud

Karma Thinley	Karma Phrin las
Karmapa Dusum Khyenpa	Karma pa Dus gsum mKhyen pa
Karmapa Mikyo Dorje	Karma pa Mi bskyod rDo rje
khandroma	mkha' 'gro ma
Khedrup Gelek Palzang	mKhas grub dGel legs dPal bzang
Khedrupje	mKhas grub rJe
Khenchen Thrangu Rinpoche	mKhan chen Khra 'gu Rin po che
Khon	Khon
Konchog Gyalpo	dKon mchog rGyal po
Kunga Nyingpo	Kun dga' sNying po
Lama Zhang	bLa ma Zhang
Lamdre	Lam 'bras
Langdarma	gLang Dar ma
lhagtong	lhag mthong
lojong	blo sbyong
Longchen Rabjam	kLong chen Rab 'byams
Lopon Sonam Tsemo	sLob dpon bSod nams rTse mo
lung	lung
Machig Labdron	Ma gcig Lab sgron
Mar	dMar
Marpa Lotsawa	Mar pa Lo tsa ba
mennag	man ngag
Milarepa	Mi la ras pa
Ngawang Kunga	Ngag dbang Kun dga'
Ngawang Legpa	Ngag dbang Legs pa
Ngawang Lodro Zhenphen Nyingpo	Ngag dbang bLo gros gZhan phan sNying po
Ngawang Lozang Gyamtso	Ngag dbang bLo bzang rGya mtsho
ngedon	nges don
Ngor	Ngor
Ngorchen Konchog Lhundrup	Ngor chen dKon mchog Lhun grub
Ngorchen Kunga Zangpo	Ngor chen Kun dga' bZang po

Ngor Phende Rinpoche	Ngor Phan bde Rin po che
Nyingma	rNying ma
Phakmo Dru	Phag mo gru
Phakmo Dru Dorje Gyaltsen	Phag mo gru rDo rje rGyal mtshan
Phenyul	'Phan yul
Radeng	Rwa sgreng
rangtong	rang stong
rangtongpa	rang stong pa
rigpa	rig pa
Rigzin Jatson Nyingpo	Rig 'dzin 'ja' tshon snying po
Rigdzin Jigme Lingpa	Rig 'dzin 'jigs med gLing pa
Rime	ris med
Rinchen Zangpo	Rin chen bZang po
Sakya	Sa skya
Sakyapa	Sa skya pa
Sakya Pandita Kunga Gyaltsen Pal Zangpo	Sa skya Pandita Kun dga' rGyal mtshan dPal bZang po
Sakya Trizin	Sa skya Khri 'dzin
Samye	bSam yas
Shakya Chogden	Shakya mChog ldan
Shangpa	Shangs pa
Shugse	Shug se
Sonam Sengge	bSod nams Seng ge
Songtsen Gampo	Srong btsan sGam po
Taglung	sTag lung
terton	gter ston
tri	khrid
Trisong Detsen	Khri srong lDe brtsan
Trophu	Khro phu
Tshal	Tshal
Tsarchen Losal Gyamtso	Tshar chen bLo gsal rGya mtsho

LIST OF TIBETAN TERMS

Tsongkhapa	gTsong Kha pa
Ü	dbUs
wong	dbang
Yamzang	g.Ya' bzang
Yel	Yel
Yeshe Tsogyal	Ye shes mTsho rgyal
yidam	yi dam
Zhalu Losal Tenchong	Zha lu bLo gsal bsTan skyong
Zhang	Zhang
zhentong	gzhan stong
zhentongpa	gzhan stong pa
zhinay	zhi gnas
zhung	gzhung

Bibliography

Atisha, *Lamp of the Path of Enlightenment: byang chub lam gyi sgron ma,* in *gdams ngag mdzod,* Lama Ngodrup and Sherab Drimey, Paro, 1979–1981, Vol 3. pp.2–8.

Chandrakirti, *Entering the Middle Way: dbu ma la 'jug pa,* Khenpo Appey, Gangtok, 1979.

Chogyal Phakpa, *Garland of Jewels* in sa skya'i bka' bum, Sakya Centre, Dehra Dun, 1992–1993, Vol. 15, pp. 315-341.

Dza Patrul Rinpoche, *The Words of My Perfect Master:* Harper Collins, London, 1992. rDza dPal sprul, *rdzogs pa chen po klong chen snying tig gi sngon 'gro'i khrid yig kun bzang bla ma'i zhal lung,* in *gsung 'bum,* Sonam T. Kazi, Gangtok, 1970–71, vol. 5, pp. 1–563.

Gampopa, *Jewel Ornament of Liberation: sGam po pa, dam chos yid bzhin nor bu thar pa rin po che'i rgyan,* Karma Chogar, Rumtek, 1972.

Gyalse Thogme Zangpo, *Thirty-Seven Practices of a Buddha's Child*: Thogs med bZang po, *rgyal ba'i sras kyi lag len sum cu so bdun ma*, in *blo sbyong nyer mkho phyogs bsgrigs*, Lanzhou, 2003, pp. 701–708.

Jamgon Kongtrul, *Instructions on the Seven Points of Mind Training*: 'Jam mgon Kong sprul, *blo sbyong don bdun ma'i khrid yig blo dman 'jug bder bkod pa byang chub gzhung lam*, in *gdams ngag mdzod*, Lama Ngodrup and Sherab Drimey, Paro, 1979–81, vol. 4, pp. 243–275.

Jetsun Drakpa Gyaltsen, *Parting from the Four Attachments*: rJe btsun Grags pa rGyal mtshan, *zhen pa bzhi bral*, in *gdams ngag mdzod*, Lama Ngodrup and Sherab Drimey, Paro, 1979–81, vol. 6, pp. 310–313.

Lama Jampa Thaye, *Rain of Clarity*, Ganesha Press, Bristol, 2006.

Maitreya / Asanga, *The Supreme Continuum Treatise*: *theg pa chen po rgyud bla ma'i bstan bcos*, Karma Chogar, Rumtek, 1972.

Mipham Rinpoche, *Gateway to Knowledge*, 4 Vols. Rangjung Yeshe Press, Kathmandu, 1997–2012.

Nagarjuna, *Letter to a Friend*, in Karma Thinley Rinpoche, *The Telescope of Wisdom*, Ganesha Press, Bristol, 2009.

Ngorchen Konchog Lhundrup, *Ornament for the Triple Tantra*: Ngor chen dKon mchog Lhun grub, *rgyud gsum mdzes par byed pa'i rgyan*, in *lam 'bras slob bshad chen mo*, Sachen International, Kathmandu, 2008, Vol.30, pp.421–656.

Ngorchen Konchog Lhundrup, *Ornament for the Triple Vision*: Ngor chen dKon mchog Lhun grub, *snang gsum mdzes par byed pa'i rgyan*, in *lam 'bras slob bshad chen mo*, Sachen International, Kathmandu, 2008, Vol.30, pp. 209–420.

Ngorchen Kunga Zangpo, *Parting from the Four Attachments*: Ngor chen Kun dga' bZang po, *zhen pa bzhi bral gyi khrid yig*, in *gdams ngag mdzod*, Lama Ngodrup and Sherab Drimey, Paro, 1979–81, vol. 6, pp. 317–342.

Sakya Pandita, *Discriminating the Three Vows*: Sa skya Pandita, *sdom pa ysum gyi rab tu dbye ha'i bstan bcos*, in sa skya'i bka' 'bum, Sakya Centre, Dehra Dun, 1992-93, Vol. 12, pp.1–98.

Sakya Pandita, *Elucidating the Thought of the Sage*: Sa skya Pandita, *thub pa'i dgongs gsal*, in *sa skya'i bka' 'bum*, Sakya Centre, Dehra Dun, 1992–93, vol. 10, pp. 1–197.

Shantideva, *Entering the Bodhisattva Conduct*: byang chub sems dpa'i spyod pa la 'jug pa, Karma Chogar, Rumtek, n.d.

Sonam Tsemo, *The General System of Tantra Sets*: bSod nams rTse mo, *rgyud sde spyi'i rnam par yzhag pa*, in *lam 'bras slob bshad chen mo*, Sachen International, Kathmandu, 2008, Vol. 23, pp. 57–216.

Tsarchen Losal Gyamtso, *The Fifty Verses on the Lama*: Tshar chen bLo gsal rGya mtsho, *bshes gnyen dum pa bsten par byed pa'i thabs shloka lnga bcu pa'i 'grel pa dngos grub rin po che'i sgo byed*, in *lam 'bras slob bshad*, Dehra Dun, 1986, vol. 8, pp. 415-465.

Zhalu Losal Tenchong, *rje btsun rdo rje rnal byor ma naro mkha' spyod kyi rdzogs rim tsa dbu ma'i khrid kyi chos nyid dngos ston zhes pa'i nyams len nyung bsdus* in the Collected Works on Vajra Yogini Sakyapa Tradition, Sachen International, Guru Lama, Kathmandu, 2003, Vol.3, pp. 421–468.

Publishing finished
in January 2023 by Pulsio
Publisher Number: 4024
Legal Deposit: January 2023
Printed in Bulgaria